RAVE REVIEWS FOR
THE CLASSR~

"Matt Vaudrey and John _____ _ for an ideal modern educator. They c~ _____. skills, like being content experts and masterful ~ _____ ~ents, with a world-class set of technology skills that incl~ _ a dizzying array of online tools and apps. They both add a social media skillset that is world class, working with thousands of educators via social media. *The Classroom Chef* is an inspiring and enlightening extension of their amazing speaking presentations. I have seen entire rooms of teachers absolutely floored by Matt and John in their element, and this book features all the best parts of their hearts and souls. It's a great read."

—Jon Corippo, CUE director of academic innovation

"John and Matt have created tasty recipes for any teacher to cook up in their math class."

—Andrew Stadel, math instructional coach

"Matt and John have compiled an inspiring and authentic account of the struggles that helped them learn how to make math class exciting. They share both general strategies and specific ideas you can immediately implement with your students to make measurable growth."

—Robert Kaplinsky, math teacher specialist

"To put it quite simply, Matt Vaudrey and John Stevens have the power to change the world. I believe so strongly in both the content and format that Matt and John deliver that I would put it this way: if you can only have one day of professional learning brought to your school or district, you need to look no further. The same is true for *The Classroom Chef*. Without a doubt, your school's educators need to read this book. As an elementary principal, I see the strategies presented by Matt and John making a difference for kids in every classroom in our school."

—Jennifer Kloczko, Star Academy coordinator

THE CLASSROOM CHEF

Sharpen Your Lessons
Season Your Classes
Make Math Meaningful

JOHN STEVENS & MATT VAUDREY

The Classroom Chef

This book is available at special discounts when purchased in quantity for use as premiums, promotions, fundraising, and educational use. For inquiries and details, contact us: shelley@daveburgessconsulting.com.

Published by Dave Burgess Consulting, Inc.
San Diego, CA
http://daveburgessconsulting.com

Cover Design by Genesis Kohler
Editing and Interior Design by My Writers' Connection

Library of Congress Number: 2016935677
Paperback ISBN: 978-0-9882176-8-3
E-book ISBN: 978-0-9882176-9-0

First Printing: March 2016

THE MENU

Introduction 1

Preparing the Kitchen 5
    Chapter 1: Finding Meaning in Math (or Any) Class 7
    Chapter 2: Giving Up on Processed Food 15

Setting the Table 31
    Chapter 3: There's No Substitute for Preparation 33

Appetizers 43
    Chapter 4: False Starts and Better Beginnings 45
    Chapter 5: Serving Up Appetizers in Your Classroom 53

Entrées 65
    Chapter 6: Barbie Zipline 67
    Chapter 7: Mullet Ratio 75
    Chapter 8: Scale Factor Billboards 81
    Chapter 9: Big Shark 85
    Chapter 10: September 11th 93
    Chapter 11: The Plating—Presentation Is Everything! 99
    Chapter 12: How to Make Your Own Entrée 113

Side Dishes 127

Chapter 13: The World Needs More Education Geeks 129

Chapter 14: Make Your Lessons Pop 137

Desserts 149

Chapter 15: Rethinking Assessment 151

The Bill 167

Chapter 16: Risks and Rewards 169

The Reviews. 179

Chapter 17: The Teacher Report Card 181

A Take-Home Container, Please! 189

The Pantry 193

Secret Ingredients (a.k.a. Works Cited) 195

Appendix A: Chefs Who Inspire Us 199

Appendix B: Salad Bar of Favorites 200

Acknowledgments 201

More From Dave Burgess Consulting, Inc. 204

About the Authors 210

DEDICATION

FOR DEDE, THE HEAD CHEF

INTRODUCTION

John George Yanko (John's grandfather, or *Dede)* only attended school through the third grade. The son of Macedonians, he immigrated to the United States during World War II to escape the thumb of the Greek government. Yanko looked for a way to support his young family.

His passion: cooking.

Yanko worked more than forty-five years as a chef—starting as a *sous-chef* at his Uncle Yanko's restaurant in Ohio, going on to run his own namesake diner in Jackson, Michigan, and later serving as the head cook at Steve's Ranch[1] in Jackson, Michigan. Even with all of those years of experience, Dede wasn't a perfect chef.

Sometimes the dough didn't knead the way it was supposed to.

Sometimes the seasonings didn't pop just right.

Sometimes—though very rarely for Dede—the oven didn't cook properly.

Dede made delicious meals for friends, family, and customers—no matter the size of the kitchen or how well it was outfitted. He worked hard to settle his family in the United States, and years later, his grandson (and co-author of the pages you are reading) became a teacher who embodied the same persistence when ingredients and conditions weren't ideal.

---

1   This was a huge step down in status and pay for him. Steve's Ranch is a little diner that saw less traffic than an Alaskan freeway.

Cooking—the kind of cooking that earns you the right to be the chef of your own restaurant—is *hard*. Neither of us will ever make *chateaubriand* as well as Dede,[2] and that's okay. Dede spent his entire life in the kitchen—making plenty of mistakes. His example and experience reassure us that, more often than not, taking risks and trying new things can lead to some epic experiences.

But this isn't a book about cooking or about Dede. *The Classroom Chef* is about what teachers experience every single year—sometimes daily, sometimes multiple times a day—as they strive to accomplish the best for their students.

We've learned from experience that teaching is *hard*.

And the longer you teach, the more evident it becomes that is there is no *best* way to teach effectively. Even more unsettling? The teaching methods that were effective for your classes last year may not work with your current group of students.

That's a tough reality to face.

Neither one of the authors was born a fantastic teacher, but we found ways to engage our students, often opening ourselves up for failure. And there has been quite a bit of failure. But amid the train wrecks and tears (and there have been lots of both), we found ways to love our profession. And we've become very proud of the hard work we do.

That pride from our work didn't come solely from the content, but rather from getting students excited about learning. Any veteran teacher will tell you it's difficult to get students excited about all topics.

We know this well; we teach math.

STANDARDS, CURRICULA, AND EDUCATIONAL TRENDS COME AND GO, BUT GOOD TEACHING IS TIMELESS.

---

2 Pronounced DEH-deh, it's a Macedonian term of endearment for "grandfather," one of the few terms successfully handed down from grandparents to grandson in our family.

Bad News and Good News

There's a real good chance that you were given this book (or bought this book) because someone told you that Common Core is a grumpy ogre and you need some tools to defend yourself and keep your job.

You'll notice as you read, however, that we don't talk about the Common Core State Standards. There's a reason for that.

This isn't a book about how to teach Common Core; it's about good teaching practices. Standards, curricula, and educational trends come and go, but good teaching is timeless. Good teaching isn't focused solely on Common Core, nor on EdTech, and definitely not on the latest trend discussed at the staff meeting.

So the bad news is that if you're looking for a book about fun Common Core activities, this ain't it. If you're looking for cool worksheets, skills for students to practice for the standardized test, and assignments that won't drive your students' parents to rant on social media, we wish you luck searching elsewhere.

However, the good news is that the teaching strategies found in these pages prepare students very well for any content standards. The skills and pedagogy we'll present here will equip you to make your classes a place where students think critically, challenge assumptions, and are excited and curious to learn about things they don't know.

Our belief is that the best lesson is like a fine meal, and you are the Classroom Chef. Unfortunately, when teaching feels hard and it seems impossible to get to every item on your to-do list, the tendency is to rely on fast food. At least, that's what we did. In our teaching careers, we initially tried to be the stereotypical, regimented types who handed out worksheets, sat at the desk, and exclusively delivered direct instruction[3] to students sitting in single-file rows of desks.

Rigid, traditional, assembly-line teaching simply didn't work for us. After looking out into a sea of seventy-two eyeballs that stared back (or into space) without a glimmer of excitement, intrigue, or curiosity,

---

3   Lecture-style teaching: To oversimplify it, the teacher talks, the students listen.

we wanted to break the mold our culture calls "normal" for our profession. We knew that if we were going to survive as educators, we needed to change the way we prepared and delivered our lessons—for our students' sakes, and for ours.

We hope you find some ideas and possibilities sprinkled throughout these pages that can work for your school, your class, and your students. You'll see that we talk openly about how difficult our careers were at various points, because we truly believe—based on the risks we were willing to take—the successes since those dark days have kept us passionate about teaching. Our excitement and pride drove each keystroke of this book.

We want *every* teacher to love this job as much as we do.

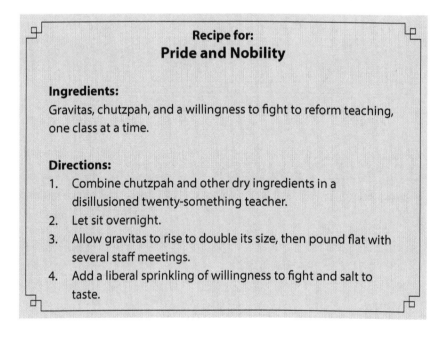

Recipe for:
Pride and Nobility

Ingredients:
Gravitas, chutzpah, and a willingness to fight to reform teaching, one class at a time.

Directions:
1. Combine chutzpah and other dry ingredients in a disillusioned twenty-something teacher.
2. Let sit overnight.
3. Allow gravitas to rise to double its size, then pound flat with several staff meetings.
4. Add a liberal sprinkling of willingness to fight and salt to taste.

Preparing the Kitchen

Mise en place is a system used by culinary experts to organize their kitchens and prepare for efficient cooking. Literally translated as "set in place," *mise en place* colloquially means to gather and arrange the ingredients and tools needed for cooking.

In a classroom, *mise en place* is essential.

Recipe for:
Chaotic Classroom

Ingredients:

1 underprepared teacher

37 rambunctious and opportunistic teenagers

31 pencils

19 notebooks, 1/3 full of paper

Directions:

Take all ingredients, mix in a blender, then put into a classroom and set on high heat for 54 minutes. Repeat for 180 days, or until burnt to a crisp.

CHAPTER 1
FINDING MEANING IN MATH
(OR ANY) CLASS

"Ariana Grande's new video is so hot."

"Your mom is so hot."

"Shut up!"

"I'm getting an iPad this weekend at Best Buy."

"Aw! Luckyyyy!"

The pre-class chatter ends suddenly as stunned middle school students watch their teacher climb onto the desk dressed in a cape and top hat.

"Prepare to be *amazed*!" he shouts, swirling the cape and leaping from desk to desk. Students roll their eyes and smile, moving their notebooks out of the way of the teacher's sneakers.

"I need a volunteer!" For some reason, he's speaking in a British accent. "You, madam! Thank you for volunteering."

Melissa looks at her neighbor, then back at the grown man standing on a desk. "Me? But I didn't say anyth—"

"Splendid! Now, up here with me, please. Hold this." Melissa grudgingly accepts a large triangle cut from cardboard.

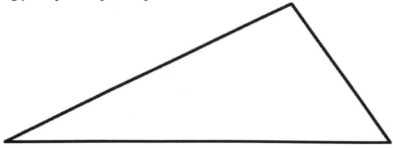

"Madam, hold this marker and do exactly as I say. I shall face the wall and reveal my magic in due time. First, write a large number 'one' on any of the angles and show the class."

Melissa puts the triangle on the desk as the other students stretch their necks to watch. The squeak of the marker on cardboard is the only sound in the room.

"Now label the other two angles 'two' and 'three,' but do NOT tell me which ones you've labeled … "

"Okayyyy?" says Melissa, playing it cool for her thirteen-year-old friends. Secretly, she's just as curious as they are. One student whispers to another, "Why are we doing this?"

Squeeeeak. Two.

Squee-eeee-eeeak. Three.

"Show the room, but do not show me! This magical cape is beginning to make my magic shoulders sweat!"

Melissa smirks and holds up the triangle to the class.

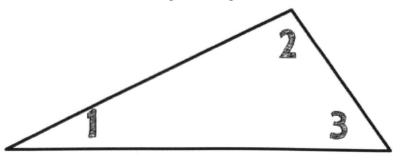

"Now this next step is very important, madam. Very important, indeed... Melissa?"

"Yeah?"

"Okay, good. You're still here. *ahem* The illusion is nearly complete! Please gently tear the triangle into three pieces, but only from the sides. Do not tear through the corners."

Melissa pauses and picks up the triangle.

"No!" shouts Leo from across the room. "The other way! Grab lower."

"Like this?" asks Melissa.

"Yeah," says Chris.

All thirty-two students watch in silence as Melissa tears apart the giant cardboard triangle.

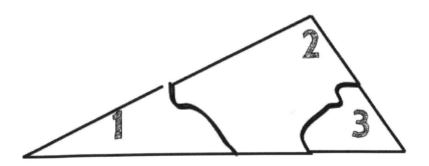

"Place one angle on the line of tape on the wall with the vertex on the dot."

Melissa crosses to the wall, raises angle one, then freezes. "Leo!" she hisses. "Help me!"

"I got it!" Angel is out of his seat before Melissa even finishes speaking. "Right here," he points to the dot on the tape and Melissa aligns the scrap of cardboard.

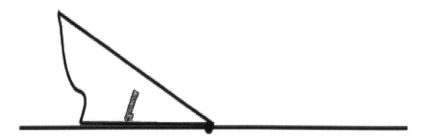

"Now the second angle, same thing." The teacher's voice is muffled by the cape and hat, but the students are fixated on Angel and Melissa.

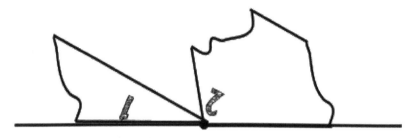

"Okay, we did it."

"Splendid!" The teacher jumps off the desk and whips around, flinging the cape in a wide arc. "And now for the finale, the prestige, *la pièce de résistance*. Watch…this…"

The teacher reaches through the air and picks up the third angle, still resting on the desk. He thrusts it into the air, stealing a peek to see all the students following his hand. *Perfect*.

Slowly, deliberately, he lowers the third angle into the gap between the other two.

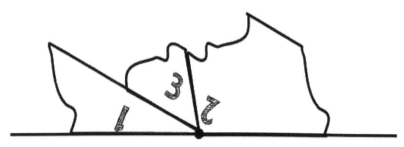

He jumps onto a chair and yells, "Ta-da! The angles in *any* triangle will *always* sum to 180 degrees! Ta-da!" He pauses and looks around the room. "I said, *Ta-da!*"

The students burst into applause. A few even say, "Whoaaaaa."

And the lesson hasn't even started yet.

IT'S OKAY IF A LESSON BOMBS. REALLY.

Contrary to what many students and teachers (maybe even you) believe, school doesn't have to be boring. It can be exciting. It can be fun. More importantly, it can be *meaningful*. Relying on that belief and a churning dissatisfaction that came from spending all day in a lifeless room with four walls and thirty-eight desks, we decided to shake things up in our classrooms. However, the road from boring to meaningful was littered with failure. In fact, between the two of us, we've had high hopes for dozens—probably *hundreds*—of class periods which completely bombed.[1] *Really* bombed. Like *senior-prank-in-the-chem-lab-gone-bad* bombed.

But through these failures, we noticed three things:

1. WE STUMBLED UPON GREAT WAYS FOR STUDENTS TO INTERACT WITH BORING CONCEPTS.

You know who wants to learn about ratios and proportions? Nobody. And not surprisingly, high percentages of hormonal teenagers also have no interest in the Latin root of the word *percent*, the concept of inverted multiplication, or using the distributive property to split up a bill.[2] But you know who wants to learn about mullets? And who loves ranking them, discussing their "mulletude," then measuring their classmates' mullets, and creating a class rank of whose haircut

---

1 Let's see...seven years of teaching comes to about six thousand lessons and some change. Oh, yeah—definitely hundreds of bombed lessons.

2 We tried all of these lessons—and they went, well, exactly how you likely think they did.

is more "mullety"?[3] Can you think of anyone who would love to send action figures and stuffed animals down a zipline?

You get where this is going.

2. OUR STUDENTS, COLLEAGUES, AND ADMINISTRATORS EASILY FORGAVE OUR FAILURES.

Even if our lesson bombed, our risks paid off in other ways. (More on that in Chapter 16.)

It would be silly to count the number of times we failed to get students to master a standard, follow through with an essential question, or reach our objective for the day. Oh, and don't bother to count the number of times we tried to do a last-minute project on the heels of a midnight idea—naïvely thinking we could pull it off the next morning if we could just get 250 feet of aluminum foil at Wal-Mart before school started.[4]

3. STUDENTS MIMICKED THE RISK-TAKING THEY SAW IN US.

Humans are a weird species. We tend to mimic the actions of those around us, even in a judgment-free culture based on respect. Risk-taking began our evolution from catastrophic failures to incremental successes, and something incredible began to happen.

Students started taking risks *of their own.*

Sure, we could've told them to follow protocol, but we knew for students to progress, they had to be challenged. We had to push them out on a limb and encourage them to take a risk.

And they *did.*

Having a safe culture that allowed, encouraged, and supported risk-taking was also helpful—especially when things went awry.

All teachers, based on our unofficial poll, were varying degrees of terrible during their first year. By their own admission, teaching was not the profession they imagined it would be. Kids didn't come in

---

3　"Business in the front; party in the back"—an 80s fashion thing. Get more info at MrVaudrey.com/mullet.

4　True story. For full details of the September 11th lesson, check out Chapter 10.

quietly, sit neatly, arrive organized, or hang on every word. As brand-new teachers, most of us assumed students would listen to our lessons as if they were sonnets read by Bill Shakespeare himself.

The lesson plans we made didn't account for the *human* aspect of our job:

- the kid who didn't sleep all night because she thought she was pregnant
- the kid who stayed up until 10:00 p.m. to take care of his siblings while mom worked her third job of the day
- the kid who would rather grow up to be a professional video gamer than anything else in the world
- the kid who fell asleep at work last night and came to school in the same clothes as yesterday[5]

These are just a few of many scenarios which shook our lesson plans to the ground. Stepping away from the traditional math class was the last thing on the minds of *these* students. Yet these are the students who stood to benefit the most from our risks.

THE ROAD FROM BORING TO MEANINGFUL WAS LITTERED WITH FAILURE.

---

5   All true stories.

Chapter 2
Giving Up on Processed Food

When we were young adults,[1] we ate any meal we could. Preparing a "great" meal in the early years of college meant grabbing the box of Velveeta Shells, a can of Hormel Chili, and a bag of Doritos to top it off. If there was no time for chili, a cut-up hot dog worked just fine. Clearly, healthy food wasn't a priority; "quick and dirty" was good enough to put calories into our bodies. Plus, prep time was a snap since the cooking instructions on the box or can usually had only four steps (or less).

Once we found women who could tolerate us, this all changed. Gone were the days of finding the cheesiest way to shovel in two thousand calories. Suddenly, we needed to research what foods paired well with one another, how different seasonings accompany certain meats and conquer the flavor of others, and the other nuances of cooking for more than one person.

Also, vegetables.[2]

---

1 Separately. The authors didn't meet until their late-twenties, which is a real shame.

2 2005: Matt's roommate, Chris—after a few months of the Velveeta and chili fare—exclaimed, "Vaudrey, I feel like garbage. Let's go buy some vegetables."

Throughout our journey, we learned more than just how to follow instructions to prepare a delicious meal we were proud to serve. Our real mission was to prepare a meal from start to finish without relying on Pinterest (or our moms).

We spent our first few years of teaching looking at textbooks (which looked a *lot* like the box of Velveeta Shells and Hormel Chili) and wondering how we could make our lessons *even a little bit* more appetizing. The Velveeta-style curriculum had a long shelf-life and worked for many years across many states, but let's be real—it looked gross.

We weren't happy with processed-food curriculum: outdated pre-printed modules for the students, a pacing guide to follow, and an entire department doing the same thing. And, from our observations of the students who had learned to hate math prior to arriving in our classrooms, it was clear a processed food math class wasn't going to cut it.

Somewhere along the line, we decided to learn how to cook math and serve it up like a fine meal. It wasn't an easy process, and it sure didn't happen during our first year on the job. When math isn't appe-

---

WE DECIDED TO LEARN HOW TO COOK MATH AND SERVE IT UP LIKE A FINE MEAL.

---

tizing, the students revolt, which usually makes new teachers cranky and leads to unfortunate memories—like kicking a cabinet.

Don't judge us too harshly for what you're about to read; this wasn't easy to type.

THE TIME JOHN KICKED A CABINET

The sole of my black Skechers dress shoe stayed firmly planted on the cabinet door, my hands clenched the top of the cabinet, as I (John) leaned back against the whiteboard trying to regain my composure.

Jesse cowered in fear from the sound of my kick against the only appropriate object where I could unleash my anger at the kids' noise level and frustration that they just weren't "getting it." The feelings of stress had been brewing for a while. It was the middle of the school year, and I couldn't take it anymore. I snapped. I kicked the cabinet behind me, releasing four months of frustration.

Suddenly, all thirty-six pairs of eyes—students who were usually unmanageably loud and repetitively disrespectful—were staring silently at Jesse or me. Rogelio, normally rambunctious and challenging, sat wide-eyed as though he had just witnessed a shooting. Alison was scared, but kept her composure. She'd watched the storm brewing. Jesse sat with his arms covering his head, knees sucked into his midsection, one eye looking through his teenage forearms—likely his standard pose to receive punishment outside of this previously safe classroom. The blood once destined for my head and my fists quickly retracted as I stared back, realizing the irreparable damage I had done.

I never scared my students again. Unfortunately, this is one of my strongest memories of my first year in the classroom.

●———————————————————————●

It pains us to recall many of the memories from those dreadful first years in the classroom. You may have similar memories. Or maybe stressed-out, frustrated moments aren't memories for you yet, but everyday occurrences. What we hope you'll understand is that the pain is worth it—valuable even—because it pushes you to make a change. In fact, it was because of the pain of those first few years that we came to realize, if we were going to stay in this profession, we *had* to get better.

We knew the fast-food curriculum wasn't going away, and district and state mandates weren't changing any time soon. Our challenge, then, was to redesign pieces of units to make them engaging and meaningful to the kids. We learned from excellent teachers—personal colleagues and those we met online—that the easiest way to manage a classroom is to keep students engaged and curious.

We needed to learn how to prepare a lesson. We needed to learn about *mise en place* and how it would look in a classroom. (We also needed to learn about our students, but we'll discuss that later.)

Preparing a Lesson

Preparing a lesson and *lesson planning* are distinctly different. Preparing a lesson takes research and new ideas to push the learning toward the objective. Lesson planning, by contrast, is the step-by-step nature of a given set of objectives.

Planning models are readily available for teachers to structure their lessons so students get good test and quiz scores to show what they've learned. We're far more interested in directing students toward the objective and far less worried about the predicted steps to get there. We want to see how deep we can dig as we move students toward the objective so that they don't just test well, but actually *learn* well.

The method of preparing a lesson includes four main processes:

- **Mark the desired outcome**

- **Investigate**

- **Scout out the day**

- **Enhance the lesson**

> **Putting our students first gives us a better start in developing a lesson centered on them.**

MARK THE DESIRED OUTCOME:
WHAT ARE STUDENTS SUPPOSED TO LEARN?

Your students don't care that today is the day you're tackling standard 8.G.A.2. And they certainly don't need thirty-nine words[3] to describe what this one picture does:

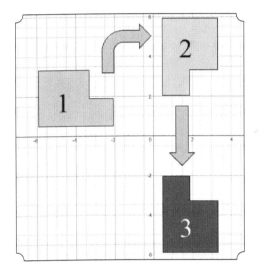

Students will care if you ask an interesting question.

Compare the two options below:

Students, on the wall there is a series of coordinate transformations. Our task is to figure out what translation, rotations, or reflections occurred to create image 3.	Whoa. Is that the same shape? What happened?

---

3   Standard 8.G.A.2: Understand that a two-dimensional figure is congruent to another if the second can be obtained from the first by a sequence of rotations, reflections, and translations; given two congruent figures, describe a sequence that exhibits the congruence between them.

Both deal with the same topic. One of the options on the previous page asks a question to get students talking, reasoning, and progressing toward the desired outcome. Yes, we still believe in teaching to standards-based learning goals. However, we don't think students need to read the whole dreadful standard. If our students walk away from this unit with only one thing, it must be meaningful. On a deeper level, the questions we ask must hook the students without compromising the content. Putting our students first gives us a better start in developing a lesson centered on them.

Start by shifting from *teacher language* into *learner language*. Explain the learning goal in the simplest way possible. If needed, pull a few students in and get their help. They don't have to know standard 8.G.A.2; they simply need to know what they'll do before they leave class today.

Develop your objective with the goal in mind—making your lesson meaningful *to students*. No matter which standards your students are supposed to learn, we can all agree experience trumps a state mandate. If the standard says students need to "write, read, and evaluate expressions in which letters stand for numbers," you—the professional educator—can determine what type of experience will best help your students learn that standard.

Mathalicious is a great resource for this, offering teachers real-world lessons to address math standards.[4] By the time the bell rings at the end of "The Bigfoot Conspiracy" lesson from Mathalicious, students can clearly express, "We figured out if people with small feet should pay less for shoes."[5]

---

4 This is the only resource we like enough to buy. Everything else we recommend is free. More on why we love Mathalicious later. Feel free to check them out if you haven't already: Mathalicious.com.

5 "Big Foot Conspiracy," Mathalicious, mathalicious.com/lessons/big-foot-conspiracy.

You won't hear any students say, "We compared equivalent ratios and proportions," but that's exactly what they did. Not only that, but our goal was masked by the lesson's overall objective of getting students to think about the fairness of shoe sales and if people with bigger feet should pay more for shoes. Our learning goal was covert. Guerilla lesson design, really. And speaking of *guerrilla* …

INVESTIGATE: DOES THE OBJECTIVE SHOW UP IN REAL LIFE OR IN SOMETHING INTERESTING?

We subscribe to the words of rap metal band Rage Against the Machine: "Know your enemy."[6] Boredom is the enemy in math class, and thousands of textbook pages are unwittingly soldiers of the enemy. In fact, much of traditional education lies in the enemy's camp. To combat the enemy, we must identify which textbook pages are our allies and leave the rest of the pages standing idly on a bookshelf.

Our allies in this fight for a meaningful math class are questions students can answer using math, resources where math appears in the real world, or interesting applications of a mathematical idea or concept. Dan Meyer, a popular voice in the movement to improve math instruction, calls this "creating a headache to which math is the aspirin." We call it *making math meaningful.*

Tomato, tom*ah*to.

Sure, you can use gimmicks to get students interested, but the value of those gimmicks quickly expires. Entertainment is not the same as engagement, and students spend most of their time at home seeking an entertaining experience. You—the teacher—have to offer a *meaningful* experience. Once we have identified an opportunity to give math meaning, we can create a narrative that adds value to the content students need to achieve the desired outcome.

---

6   Yep, we know; it's unusual to quote hard rock legends in a book about math education.

Scout out the Day: How can I craft a narrative or flow?

Keep in mind that we're preparing a lesson, not lesson planning. We're not typing out a play-by-play of events. Although, truth be told, we have done this plenty of times in our careers with mixed results. Whether mid-lesson or reflecting at the end of the day, Robert Burns was right when he said, "The best laid schemes of mice and men oft go awry, and leave us nothing but grief and pain, for promised joy!" If I'm scripting out my entire lesson without room for the natural flow of a class, what value am I adding to the material?

This is a real question we need to consider when preparing a lesson.

The status quo model of direct-instruction lectures falls short of crafting a narrative. By contrast, when the class is focused on a story, a question, or a weird idea, discussion flows naturally with the content propelling it.

For example, in the graphics for the lesson about solving systems of equations (Figures 1 and 2), the guiding question—"Which Is Cheaper?"—is present at each step. In pursuit of finding which item is cheaper, students explore several mathematical concepts:

- Define important information

- Ignore extraneous information

- Find the unit rate

- Apply the unit rate to multiple inputs

- Plot points, draw a line, note intercepts

- Infer why the intercept is important

- Translate what this means for real-life applications

Figure 1

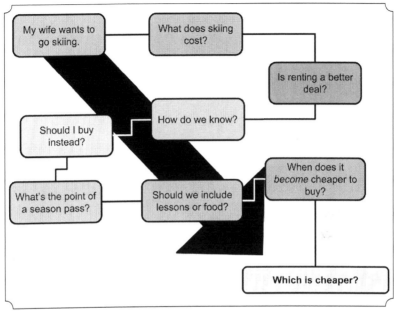

Figure 2

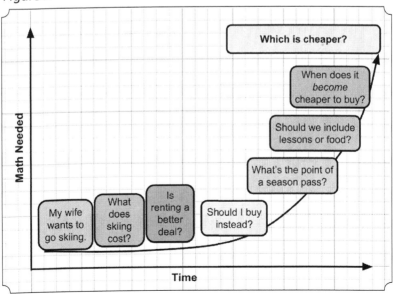

Some teachers are required to write out and submit lesson plans on a weekly basis. We've been down that road and have found the paperwork to be a waste of time for everyone involved.[7] Worse, because teachers get so focused on the paperwork, the lesson plans end up dry, lacking spice, and devoid of rich context. Nevertheless, most teachers will take at least ten minutes to scrawl out on paper the learning goal and some steps of the lesson—ten minutes which could have been better spent *preparing a lesson* instead of *writing a lesson plan*.

We have also attended trainings which encouraged us to write out prompting questions ahead of time and make sure to use them at specific points in the lesson. In practice, we've discovered that a detailed script of a lesson robs the class of the spontaneity which makes teaching such a joy.

Creating a *flow* of the class—instead of a script—leaves opportunity for questions to drive instruction without derailing the desired outcomes.

Enhance: What's my least favorite part of this lesson?

The other—and perhaps more concerning—issue with detailed lesson planning and scripting is that it doesn't allow for changing the recipe during a lesson. Ask any teacher who has taught the same lesson more than once in a day if they tweak the lesson from class to class. Of course they do. It's rare *not* to find flaws in a lesson the first time you present it. You're allowed to enhance, tweak, or completely redesign the lesson for the next class period.

Likely we've all been in English classes where our peers have proofread our essays, provided us with a fresh perspective, and potentially lifted us out of writing ruts. Interestingly, the section of our essay our

---

7   For those teachers in this situation, talk to your administrator about the shift from lesson planning to preparing a lesson. Feel free to have them email Matt. He loves emails.

peers found as the weakest was often the least exciting part for us to write.

But as teachers, we rarely seek the opinions of others on our lesson plans. Or we only ask opinions from those we know won't hurt our feelings by insisting we scrap the lesson altogether. When we do reach out for input, it's usually for affirmation, not for improvement. Small wonder that some teachers shrink further and further into their own classrooms as years go by.

What if we asked for feedback honestly, candidly, and often? Much like players in pickup basketball games begin to coach each other or writing groups offer authentic feedback, an honest professional teaching cohort can provide new perspective and improve even the best-prepared lesson.

While it may feel risky to seek feedback from other educators or our students, the rewards far outweigh the potential hurt feelings of someone criticizing your work. We've both experienced the fear that accompanies opening oneself to others' insights on our work, but embracing outside feedback has empowered us to take bigger risks and seek bigger rewards from the lessons we teach.

ASK FOR HELP WITH ENHANCING YOUR LESSONS

After seven years in the classroom, I (John) took a job as a technology coach for my school district. One of many advantages is that I get to be a part of hundreds of classrooms around the district and affect a larger scale of change.

However, being out of the classroom certainly has its disadvantages—most considerably the lack of daily student interaction and gradual loss of content knowledge. When Mr. Hansen, a math teacher at one of my high schools, asked me to teach a lesson incorporating technology into a math classroom, I couldn't say yes quickly—or enthusiastically—enough.

"Woohoo!!! I get to go back into the classroom!"

One problem though. I'd never taught the topic: deriving the equation of a circle. Not to fear; this is when the fun began. Immediately, I sent a message to my Twitter support group and asked for help with enhancing a lesson I had drawn up:

John Stevens
@Jstevens009   ⚙ Following

#MTBoS, looking to help a geometry teacher introduce the derivation of the equation of a circle. Help? desmos.com/calculator/sb4… @desmos

RETWEET   LIKE
1   1

8:26 PM - 1 Apr 2014

[8]

And, of course, the response was nearly immediate and incredibly awesome:

Jen Silverman
@jensilvermath   ⚙ 👤 Follow

@a_mcsquared @Jstevens009 @Desmos Yes, two of my suite of 16 conics applets. geogebratube.org/material/show/…

RETWEET   LIKE
1   1

5:23 AM - 2 Apr 2014

↩   ⇄   ♥   •••

---

8   #MTBoS, which we will explain in detail later, is like a Bat-Signal for a room of helpful math teachers on Twitter. Wait, you haven't joined Twitter yet? C'mon!

Gulp! Some of the best feedback—pushback—is often the toughest to swallow. Bree (respectfully) questioned the flow and intent of the lesson and I appreciated it (see comment below).

John Stevens @Jstevens009 · 5 Apr 2014
@btwnthenumbers Thanks for the reply, Bree. If you have time, I'd love your feedback on the lesson:
docs.google.com/presentation/d...

View details

Bree Pickford-Murray @btwnthenumbers · 6 Apr 2014
@Jstevens009 hard to tell from the slides, but seems like you jump to the formula pretty quickly. We have Ss play w/ #'s for a while first.

John Stevens @Jstevens009 · 6 Apr 2014
@btwnthenumbers elaborate on "a while". I'm hoping to have kids use desmos for a good 5-10 minutes to manipulate the sliders for circles

Bree Pickford-Murray
@btwnthenumbers   Following

@Jstevens009 "A while"=about 4-5 problems They find all lattice points at -blah- distance from a point & sketch circle. Work is all by hand.

LIKE
1

2:12 PM - 6 Apr 2014

Bree Pickford-Murray @btwnthenumbers · 6 Apr 2014
@Jstevens009 I have doubts about the sliders in @Desmos for this kind of derivation. Not saying it wouldn't work, just saying I don't know.

John Stevens @Jstevens009 · 6 Apr 2014
@btwnthenumbers @Desmos I appreciate the pushback. I'll take a look at what the lesson is again and see if I can allow for more play time

Bree's feedback about getting students to work with the math really made me think about the connections that could be better formed to match the needs of the students and the topic. Thank you, Bree!

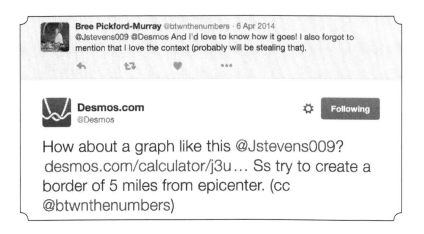

Not only did this experience increase my already strong love of Twitter, but by lowering my guard and being vulnerable to criticism, I discovered a number of professionals from around the country who offered support and resources that would help me impact the students and their understanding of the desired outcome. Matt, Hedge, Bree, Jen, Desmos,[9] and Jed[10] all lent a hand to ensure the lesson went smoothly.

While John's story emphasizes the use of Twitter as a resource for improving a lesson, it also highlights the power of asking for help from a community. Seeking out new voices and different opinions improves the design of your lesson.

---

9 Desmos.com, the free online graphing calculator that has quickly become a favorite of math teachers around the world.

10 On Twitter @mrvaudrey, @approx_normal, @btwnthenumbers, @jensilvermath, @desmos, and @mathbutler, respectively.

Not noted in the story above was a civil engineer from New York who saw the tweet and offered his assistance. It's pretty amazing when someone from the other side of the country *outside the field of education* is willing to lend a hand to make fifty-one minutes more meaningful to a group of students he will never meet.

Prior to sending the tweet request, the lesson might have rated about a 6.4 out of 10. However, seeking support to improve the lesson raised it to a solid 8.3 out of 10. A lot of improvement can still be made to it— as with any lesson—but the students were engaged with the material and enjoyed the lesson's method of deriving the equation of a circle.

As soon as the first lesson ended, John and Mr. Hansen immediately reflected on how to improve it. By the end of the day, the kids "got it." Formative assessment—a quick Socrative[11] quiz—proved they could derive the equation of a circle; the desired outcome was defined and achieved.

Now What? Preparing Your Kitchen

Ponder these questions as you prepare your own lesson:

- What are some ways you can expand your reach with the content?

- Who are some people you can lean on for improvements or advice?

- Is there something new you have learned that you've been dying to try?

---

11 Socrative.com is a free and simple tool to formatively assess students who have access to a smartphone, tablet, laptop, or desktop. It's pretty amazing.

- Who are some experts on this topic you can consult?

- What profession uses this topic? Can you secure a guest speaker?[12]

Take a moment to create a recipe for success by preparing your educational kitchen in a way that is meaningful and engaging to you. And just for fun, what was your recipe for disaster during your first year(s) of teaching? After joining in the mayhem of our early teaching experiences, surely you were reminded of a personal genuine failure worthy of sharing. Using the card found at classroomchef.com/recipe-card, create a recipe that helps you laugh at yourself and gives first-year teachers some common ground.

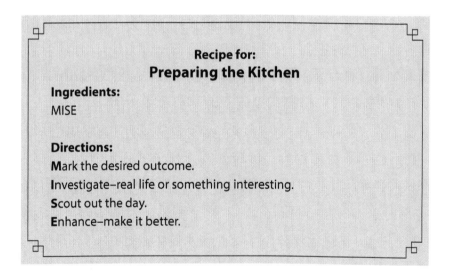

Recipe for:
Preparing the Kitchen

Ingredients:
MISE

Directions:
Mark the desired outcome.
Investigate–real life or something interesting.
Scout out the day.
Enhance–make it better.

---

12 Expand the circle of your guest speakers to include those who can't physically come to your classroom. Free video-conferencing services like Google Hangout and Skype allow you to connect your students with the world at large.

SETTING THE TABLE

When we enter a fancy restaurant on our annual spend-too-much-on-dinner anniversary date, Andrea and I (Matt) both stand a little taller. Dim lighting creates private halos over each booth and smooth jazz hums in the background.

"Mr. Vaudrey? Right this way." The black-clad host guides us to a plush booth set with black napkins and a freshly printed drink menu. Somehow, I maintain the illusion that I'm accustomed to tables without ketchup bottles and sticky spots. My first thought is always, "I do not belong here."

Before we can even look at the menu, the house sommelier recommends a wine pairing for the chef's featured dish, and the manager stops by our table to wish us another happy year of marriage and to give us a gift card. Every year, without fail, Andrea turns to me before the drinks even arrive and says, "This place is nice. We have *got* to come back here."

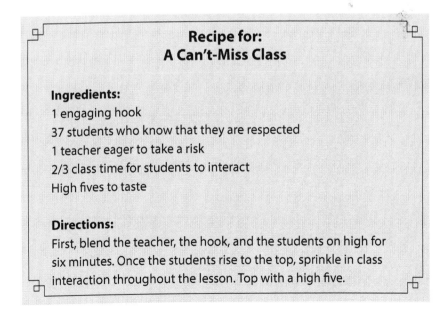

Recipe for:
A Can't-Miss Class

Ingredients:
1 engaging hook
37 students who know that they are respected
1 teacher eager to take a risk
2/3 class time for students to interact
High fives to taste

Directions:
First, blend the teacher, the hook, and the students on high for six minutes. Once the students rise to the top, sprinkle in class interaction throughout the lesson. Top with a high five.

Chapter 3
There's No Substitute for Preparation

Does the fork go on the left or right? What about the salad and dessert forks? The butter knife? How should the napkin be placed?

Setting a table in such a way that invites diners to enjoy an exquisite four-course meal takes some effort. With so many pieces of flatware on the table, it may seem like no big deal to forget to put one out—until dessert comes and your guests have nothing left to eat with but their fingers. And you're serving *crème brûlée*.

In the same way, it's nearly impossible to hide mistakes if you fail to set the "classroom table" properly; your students will notice.

If you forget to copy both sides of the handout, they'll smell it in the air.

If you rush through the problems without creating the answer key, they'll see it in your eyes.

Most importantly, if you aren't passionate about what you're serving up, they'll know.[1]

---

1 All of which we have done.

Over time, we've gradually become better at preventing these classroom-kitchen nightmares. The key is to prepare your kitchen and methodically set the table. But there are times when the preparation becomes too hard and complacency sets in. Even though technology has made it more difficult to accept complacency in the classroom,

---

IT'S NEARLY IMPOSSIBLE TO HIDE MISTAKES IF YOU FAIL TO SET THE "CLASSROOM TABLE" PROPERLY; YOUR STUDENTS WILL NOTICE.

---

it's still a very real threat. According to the Alliance for Excellence in Education, "Roughly half a million educators either move [change teaching jobs] or leave the profession each year." And that doesn't include the ones who stay but develop an increasingly sour taste in their mouths for the field of education.

At some point, we've both wanted to quit teaching.

THE TIME MATT YELLED AT KIDS

One Wednesday during my first year, I woke up late. The worksheet I needed for class was unfinished, still open on my classroom computer, but not printed or copied onto the goldenrod paper (because a goldenrod worksheet is much more engaging than a white worksheet). My first-period class was waiting outside the classroom door as I arrived.

"You're laa-aaate!" Jennifer sang with a smirk.

"I know," I growled in reply, thinking my cold response and menacing scowl would wipe that smile off her face.

It didn't.

I unlocked the classroom and led them inside. But before the warm yellow light had even filled the room, they were hassling one another:

"What's the homework from last nigh—"

"Do you have a tissu—"

"You're in my seat, assho—"

"Are you going out with Bri—?"

"Why didn't you text me last n—?"

I'd had it already.

As a "B" student throughout high school and college, I hadn't had to work very hard to succeed. Success in teaching, however—unlike success in calculus and Spanish—wasn't tied to effort or desire. Only the passage of time would improve my craft, and Father Time appeared to be in no hurry.

Months—*months*—of hard work, staying up late, getting up early, and Googling "how to manage a classroom" had led to this point at 8:01 a.m. that November morning. I was three months closer to the end of the year, but no closer to building a classroom that students respected. No closer to enjoying coming to work. No closer to being the positive role model I'd hoped to be.

I'd never been so frustrated in my entire life. The antsy feeling beneath the soles of my feet made me want to scream and punch and cry all at once. I turned my anger to the last place I should: my first-period students.

"Siddown!" I clenched both fists at my sides and kicked the stool next to my desk. It fell with a *crack* onto the thin carpet.

"Whoa! Why did he do that?"

"Why did you do that, mister?"

"Shuttup! He's mad!"

I didn't wait for them to settle down. My fists hung heavy on the ends of my arms as I seethed through gritted teeth.

"In *this* classroom, we raise our *hands* before we *speak!*" I shrieked.

Panting, I surveyed the room of thirty-five teenage faces for a long moment. Furious, I made angry eye contact with my "frequent flyers"—the ones who get demerits every day. That was the angriest, meanest-sounding sentence I'd said in my entire life. Never in twenty-three years had I used that tone with anybody, but here I'd done it purposefully to get students to obey me.

Normally, I'm a smiley individual. I laugh and joke often, and my friends call me a party-starter. I'm glad none of them were in the room to see me like this.

I limped through the remaining forty minutes with a forgettable lesson on the coordinate plane. During lunch, I photocopied the finally completed worksheet onto goldenrod paper and, as the last student trotted out at 2:55, I locked the door and turned out the lights before turning back toward my desk.

My shoes dragged across the thin, faded carpet, past five rows of tables to my teacher desk, where I collapsed into the chair with a *fwump*. In my line of vision, the trashcan under the desk held a paper with a broken pen and ink spilled all over it. Saul had placed the broken pen face-up on my chair during third period, hoping I would sit on it.

I really hope I'm not sitting in ink right now, but I'm too tired to stand up and check. This day couldn't possibly have gone worse.

The night before, Andrea had a dinner with her grad school friends. When they asked my occupation, I'd smugly replied, "I'm a Youth Ministry major teaching middle school math." They'd grinned. I'd felt good about myself.

Not even twenty-four hours later, I yelled at thirteen-year-olds. Screamed at children.

That moment—2:56 p.m. on that Wednesday in November—I realized *this is not the job I wanted.*

Slowly, I leaned forward and rested my forehead on a pile of ungraded Percentage Projects. Both arms hung limply from my shoulders. With my foot, I slid the trashcan below my face in case I cried or vomited—or both.

Weak, tired, and miserable, I allowed myself to focus on the thought which had been lurking in the back of my mind for eighty-seven days: *It can't be this hard to be a good teacher.*

And then the most troubling realization of all: *If this is what it takes to be a good teacher, I don't want to be a good teacher.*

In fact, if this is what it takes—I closed my eyes—*I don't want to be a teacher.*

CLASS CULTURE STARTS AT 7:20 A.M.

Good restaurant owners work hard to prepare the kitchen and set the table before patrons arrive. They know that from the way the host greets people as they enter, to the cleanliness of the floors, to the tidiness of the tables, to the proper place settings laid out in a neat and orderly manner—the *details* determine customers' dining experiences—and whether or not they'll return for another meal.

A classroom is the same way. Your class culture begins long before students walk through our doors.

How do you greet students as they enter the room?

How do you make the classroom a safe place?

How can you make students curious about the day?

What does the physical layout of the room tell students about your class?

Can you adjust the physical layout of the room to make it more useful for the lesson?

> YOUR CLASS CULTURE BEGINS
> LONG BEFORE STUDENTS WALK
> THROUGH OUR DOORS.

WHY WOULD SOMEONE WALK THROUGH OUR DOORS IF THEY WEREN'T LEGALLY REQUIRED TO ATTEND CLASS?

In 2010, each new teacher in Moreno Valley USD received a copy of Harry and Rosemary Wong's *The First Days of School*.[2] Some of the chapters are outdated, but Matt re-reads it every August, asking himself the questions above to help him focus his classroom on students. Throughout the book, the authors comb through the proper steps of making a classroom safe and welcoming. According to the Wongs, students feel safe when they know what to expect; with routine, humans are comfortable. "Students want to know who you are as a person and if you will treat them with respect. It is important that you allay any fears they may have about being in your class. The best way to do this is to smile, exude caring, and communicate positive expectations."

It's not a new idea. For thousands of years, authors have been proclaiming, "Preparation leads to victory," though admittedly often in a bit more sinister tone. For example, here's Sun Tzu from *The Art of War*:

> *Thus it is that in war the victorious strategist / only seeks battle after the victory has been won, / whereas he who is destined [for] defeat / first fights and afterwards looks for victory.*

Putting aside the language of *battle* and *defeat*, this ancient text claims what all teachers know: If you roll into class hoping to teach on the fly, you're screwed. If you prepare first, your chances of "victory" are much higher, and students will respond. Students *must* know what to expect before they arrive in class, and you—the teacher—must prepare them.

---

2 If you're about to start your career, go buy it now. It's the Bible for teachers.

The routine matters more than any lesson you teach.

In *Switch*, a must-read book by Chip Heath and Dan Heath, the authors describe Natalie Elder, an elementary school principal in Tennessee, who models setting the table on a whole-school level.

While the entire book is about "how to change things when change is hard," Elder's role in changing the culture of a tumultuous school into a place where students walked quietly to class is phenomenal. "Her real goal was to transform chaos into calm. In her judgment, the trouble began the moment students arrived at school. If students were rowdy by 8:30 a.m., Elder reasoned, there wasn't much hope for the rest of the day. She resolved to conquer the morning by creating a series of consistent routines that would settle the students and prepare them to learn."

The Heath brothers dive deeper into the story and share how she welcomed students as they got dropped off at school with valet service (a personal escort from their car to the cafeteria by one of the teachers), started every day the same way, had a "brief (school) lesson in character education," and sent the students off to class with arms folded behind them, ready to learn. The routine she created changed the entire school culture.[3]

Take this down to a classroom level. What does your culture feel like? Pay attention to the habits you build even before the bell rings. Of course, the first few years of teaching are riddled with a focus on the habits of students once they are *in* the classroom rather than the habits they bring *to* the classroom before the bell rings. This focus on content over culture is natural early in a teacher's career. Managing class culture comes second, though content and culture are closely related.[4]

---

3   To be clear, too much structure begins to impede on a student's natural curiosity. Let kids be kids within the expectations you provide.

4   Matt's first master teacher, Kelli Medley, said, "It doesn't matter how good your lesson is if the students aren't listening."

When our students enter the room, our first interactions communicate volumes to them. Rather than shake hands or give fist bumps to *every* student who walks in the door, give each student a custom greeting. Maybe Freddy loves the fist bump, and Samantha is ready for her high five every morning, but Eduardo prefers a head nod. Giving students a choice in their social interactions, as well as their academics, is one powerful way to establish a culture of respect for the individuals in your classroom.

Class culture is about far more than how you welcome students into class. Some teachers personally hand out papers as a way of controlling the pace of the day, which has some advantages, such as being able to pass them out quickly and without distraction, rather than a hormone-infused teenager parading through the room. It also allows for quick, one-on-one conversations with students.

Routines and expectations will change in your classroom over time. For example, you may decide to put handouts (when they are necessary) on a table and designate a student to pick up the appropriate number for his or her group, row, or side of the room. Putting students in charge of this task makes it easier for the teacher to address individual students, take attendance, or just spend more time greeting the kids as they come in for the day. Consider these routines to "set the table" for your students:

- Shake hands (or fist bump or high five) with students every day when they arrive.[5]

- Set the handouts (or other materials) on a desk or table by the front door—and don't move that table. Students learn to check the table every day. An empty table means *nothing to grab.*

- Use the same start-of-class routine every day, right when class starts. For example, students take out their notebooks and copy

---

5   This has the double bonus of establishing face time and touch with every student and reminding them that they're entering your space and you're choosing to welcome them into it.

the Essential Question from your board into their notes; take out last night's assignment for a stamp; read while the teacher takes attendance and does a lunch count; sharpen pencils; open the textbook to the page number written in red on the top right corner of the board.

- With ninety seconds left in class, students pack up and stand to practice multiplication facts.

- Train your students to listen to your full instructions without moving. Then when you say, "Go," they can spring into action.

- Instead of cold-calling students—or asking the whole class and waiting for raised hands—play a one-minute song, prompting students to talk to their partners. While the song plays, tap five or six students and say, "I'm calling on you." When the song ends, call on each student, *but give no indication if they're correct or not.*[6] See if you have consensus on the sum of 12 and 20 or the prime minister of Malaysia or whatever.

After nearly a decade of teaching, we've both found ways to enjoy our jobs. We love children and teaching and are trying our best to build a noble profession *without* yelling, no matter how hard it may be. The path out of despair—the reason we're writing this book—resulted from people we trust asking us questions that made us think and showing us great examples of fun learning environments. That's what we're hoping to give you here.

Let's get to it. The table is set.

---

6   For more on that, see Jamie Duncan's section in Entrées.

Finally, They're Starting to Get It!

Kylia rang her bell during Review Jeopardy one day. "Is this right?"

"Show the class," I (Matt) responded.

"Yeah, but is it right?" Kylia was still holding her whiteboard up to her shoulders, hiding it.

True to form, I said, "*Pfff.* I don't know."

Next to her, Myles said, "Just show it. The class will tell you if it's wrong."

"Yeah!" shouted Hillary, across the room. "Take a risk!"

I teared up a little bit. After years of hard work to create a place where incorrect answers were a welcome step in understanding, my students were beginning to understand:

They're not wrong answers, they're just not correct yet.

After hearing me say it dozens—maybe hundreds—of times, they weren't just parroting back what I'd taught them—they were starting to value taking risks.

Appetizers

Bite-sized dishes served before the meal at a restaurant whet the appetite, complement the meal, and (let's get real) encourage diners to spend just a little more. The chef knows that sending out an *antipasti* plate, or even a few breadsticks, will give her a little more time in the kitchen to perfect the main course. While tasty, those breadsticks can also be so filling that finishing the main course can be a challenge. The trick: offering the right flavors in the right proportion.

The same is true of your classroom appetizers. The goal of the ideal appetizer is to be immediately engaging; no need to bring false hype into the classroom. It doesn't need to entertain and certainly doesn't need to incorporate technology. As you consider ways to build your own appetizers (regardless of content area), focus on how these few minutes of introduction can serve the day's lesson.

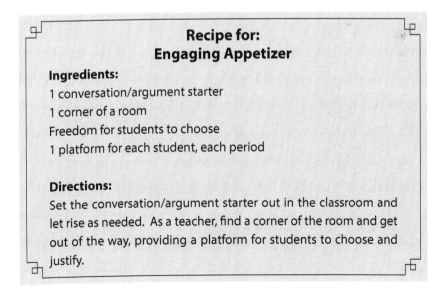

Recipe for:
Engaging Appetizer

Ingredients:
1 conversation/argument starter
1 corner of a room
Freedom for students to choose
1 platform for each student, each period

Directions:
Set the conversation/argument starter out in the classroom and let rise as needed. As a teacher, find a corner of the room and get out of the way, providing a platform for students to choose and justify.

Chapter 4
False Starts and Better Beginnings

For many years, we fought the same battles every day: "All right class, good morning. Go ahead and solve the three problems at the board. Remember, we worked on these yesterday, so you should be rock stars when it comes to applying the exponent rules. As you do that, I'll be walking around to stamp your agenda, checking to make sure that you got a paren—Tonya! I said *siddown*, Tonya! Now!—parent signature on page thirty-seven. If you need help at the end of the day, please see me during lunch or after school for tutoring. OK, questions? Great. Go ahead and get started."

Tonya doesn't want to sit down, Jason forgot his planner *again*, Daisy broke her pencil and needs to sharpen it *right now* (plus, Nico sits near the pencil sharpener and she wants to touch his hair), Darin really wants to get an "A" in this class, but Gina won't ever shut up.

All the while, what we really wanted was for our kids to answer the warm-up so we could take attendance and get the class moving.

We're quite glad there is no video footage from the early years in the classroom. Classroom management and class routines go hand in hand, and they're universally the weakest tools in a new teacher's toolbox. Thankfully, starting your class well doesn't have to be a battle

> ## CLASSROOM MANAGEMENT AND CLASS ROUTINES GO HAND IN HAND, AND THEY'RE UNIVERSALLY THE WEAKEST TOOLS IN A NEW TEACHER'S TOOLBOX.

that makes you want to walk out your classroom door. Low-barrier, risk-taking appetizers can help establish your start-of-class routine. Training your students for these kinds of appetizers take time, and the class culture will be slow to change, but the payoff is *way* worth it.

While we began this appetizer process prior to the invention of Would You Rather? and Estimation 180, among a plethora of other palatable options,[1] we found that these tools were great ways to get kids excited about the day's lesson. But they're only the beginning. In the next few pages, we want to explore and explain a few of our kick-starters.

Our appetizers started out as current event videos or a silly game to get the kids laughing, thinking, or talking. However, this practice quickly evolved into something heartier.

ARE APPETIZERS A WASTE OF CALORIES AND CONTENT?

Appetizers are my (John's) least favorite portion of a restaurant menu. They are regularly overpriced, way too common, and lack connection to the meal I'm about to order. Please don't tell me spinach

---

1 WouldYouRatherMath.com and Estimation180.com. Have we mentioned how this is a great time to be a teacher? Stuff like this is free online.

and artichoke dip should get me excited about fettuccine alfredo with garlic bread and a side salad. I'm not wasting my money (or stomach space) on your calorie bomb, thank you very much.

During my early years of teaching, my distaste for classroom appetizers mirrored my distaste of restaurant appetizers. The warm-up was disjointed from the objective of the current lesson, was usually monotonous, and lacked the one purpose I needed most: a bridge between what they were doing before class and the exciting lesson I was about to give.

I can't tell you how many times I lost a class in the first five minutes. "Good morning, class. Remember yesterday? When we solved a system of equations by substitution? Yes, you do remember; it's in your notes. There are five systems on the board, I'll give you one minute for each. Take out last night's work, then I'll take attendance and we'll get started."

I wish this was an exaggeration, but it was the truth. For far too long, my students solved warm-up questions from the board so I could take attendance, and grill Jesse for failing to do his homework yet again. My appetizers were a filler, a waste of space.

I got sick of it, so I tried to find a better way.

OR ARE APPETIZERS THE BEST THING EVER?

Appetizers are my (Matt's) wife's *favorite* part of the menu. She regularly orders appetizers as her main course. Sometimes we will go on a date and just order appetizers.

Well…appetizers and drinks.

We like to sample a variety of tasty morsels from a variety of regions or palates.

Tri-meat sampler? Yes, please.

Street tacos? *¡Claro que sí!*

Sliders, mozzarella sticks, *and* fried calamari? Don't mind if I do!

However, I'm always back in my own kitchen later that evening making a sandwich, because a meal based entirely on appetizers doesn't satisfy.

FROM BREADSTICKS TO MEATBALLS: FOURTH-YEAR TEACHING

The state test was over. Which meant I (Matt) had until summer—five weeks—to structure my math class however I wanted. We did Mullet Ratio, we did Barbie Bungee, we did Big Shark and Bucky the Badger and—eventually—I began to check out. It was the last week of May, and students were getting restless. Many stopped bringing backpacks or pencils. So I began to structure a class full of bite-sized tasks that took twenty minutes, and we'd do four in a row.

You see where this is going.

The same diversity of tastes that made my date night so delicious created chaos for my eighth graders. There was no continuity, no flow or connection between four disparate activities, so it seemed to them like wasting time.

Which it absolutely was.

WHEN WARM-UPS STOPPED SUCKING: THIRD-YEAR TEACHING

Looking back, we cringe at the number of instruction hours that were lost because we didn't know how to grab our students' attention and—more importantly—their *trust* in the first thirty seconds of the period. Sometimes the lesson introduction took up more than half the class period, forcing us to rush through the part of the lesson we'd actually prepared well.

Early in our careers, we'd hang our heads, sigh, and wonder, *Isn't there a way to fix this?* While we had no absolute solutions, reaching out to the Math Twitter Blog-o-Sphere—or #MTBoS—provided the abundant, engaging variety of appetizers our students deserved.

One recurring suggestion was, "Get kids to argue—with math as their foundation."

Intriguing.

In history, science, and English classes, kids were always having discussions about the content without explicitly citing the content (or so it seemed). For once in our teaching career, we wanted a kid to stand up in class and say, "No! The cash price is a better deal because the percentage cash back on a credit card purchase doesn't outweigh the APR!"

We wanted to start a "math fight," so we began to pit students against each other by dividing them over silly things. These tasks became

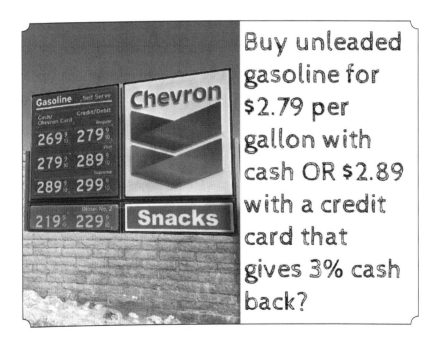

known as "Would You Rather?"

When John first posed this question as the warm-up—dropped in cold, with no warning—kids immediately picked sides and started holding their ground on their decisions. Tommy blurted out, "Paying with a credit card is stupid because you're always gonna have to pay interest," at which Lauren got mildly offended and barked back with, "Only if you're too lazy to pay your bill on time! Otherwise, paying with

---

A LONG APPETIZER IS NOT A TIME-SUCK, BUT A GENUINE OPPORTUNITY TO BUILD INTEREST FOR A LESSON.

---

credit actually makes you money in the long run. I'm going with the credit card because it's obviously better." Before the class turned into an all-out melee, we determined who was in which camp and invited a couple of other rebuttals to add flavor to the discussion. The best part of the fourteen-minute discussion about percentages and interest rates was watching as kids argued their points without realizing (maybe) they were speaking with such a heavy math accent that Euclid himself would've shed a tear of joy.

We're not recommending that every single day begin with an argument. In fact, some days, a reflection of yesterday's lesson is exactly what your students need. The point is this: You have options to bring meaning to a math class—and that's a huge benefit over being relegated to the monotony of many traditional classroom appetizers.

If you want to see rock-solid appetizers, visit a prekindergarten class for a day. For example, when the class was starting to learn about the letter "B," John's son's teacher brought in a butterfly—yes, an actual butterfly—so the kids could build synapses around what a butterfly is and the fact that its name starts with the letter B. Sure, she could've gone to the trusty ol' Internet and searched through thousands of images for a butterfly, but it doesn't have the same effect. Those kids not only made a connection between the letter B and a butterfly, but they also made a deeper connection with their teacher.

This pre-kindergarten teacher took the time to prepare an appetizer that would lock the kids in from the time they entered class until it was time for lunch. We should want the same experience for our kids, whether they're four years old, fourteen years old, or older.

A long appetizer is not a time-suck, but a genuine opportunity to build interest for a lesson. While a letter-B butterfly is cute and an incredibly effective appetizer, most of us can't bring in a military-issue tank to introduce World War II. Most of us don't have the means to take students to a rendition of *Hamlet* prior to reading Shakespeare. In fact, many teachers have content so theoretical or analytical that a direct connection to real life would smell like a farce.

So what?

Try something anyway. Your attempt to breathe life into a dusty topic will, at worst, be a welcome distraction to break up the day, or, at best, forge a deeper relationship between the content and the students.

MAKE IT MOUTHWATERING

Jin-Le throws a rock off the top of the Grand Canyon. The path of the rock follows the parabolic path $-16t^2 + 2200$. How long until his rock strikes the ground?[2]

Students smell this processed food immediately. They—and most of us—have no appetite to dive into this before digging into the day's content. As an appetizer, it's comparable to common mozzarella sticks. They're on every menu, typically underwhelming, and take too much time to consume. *Meh.*

---

2 Because kids are always wondering about parabolic functions as they throw stuff from tall places. Frank Noschese (and others) call this "pseudo-context," and while the Jin-Le problem isn't an exact quote from a textbook, every book we've seen has some variation of this problem.

But then there are those menu items which buck tradition with a bit of flair—mozzarella balls coated with crushed sea salt crackers and served with an avocado-lime dipping sauce. You don't just gulp down these creations so you can move on to the next course. You enjoy the

> **Rather than using the appetizer to get your students comfortable in their seats, use it to give them a hunger that only seconds and thirds will satisfy.**

unique effort that went into them. You savor each bite. And, if your friends are very lucky, you share it (only a bite or two) with the people around you.

Students derive the same enjoyment from a carefully prepared classroom appetizer. They will savor it, enjoy the unique effort put into it, and share it with the students around them. Teachers have to teach them to focus on the process instead of the result; many students won't take kindly to a sudden detour off the paved road to the right answer. Rather than using the appetizer to get your students comfortable in their seats, use it to give them a hunger that only seconds and thirds will satisfy.

CHAPTER 5
SERVING UP APPETIZERS IN YOUR CLASSROOM

A good appetizer starts with taking an idea and watching it flourish. Jot down an upcoming lesson and brainstorm ideas about a unique way to start the lesson. Don't be afraid to Google it. Head to ClassroomChef.com/links for resources and download our "Would You Rather?" handout. Check out Fishing4Tech.com/mtbos or search the blogs of other math teachers. Technology makes it easier than ever to find and share resources. Make sure you doctor up the recipe before serving it. Students can tell when you're reheating somebody's leftovers.

During our Classroom Chef training at conferences, we provide teachers with a list of appetizers. Our goal is to make sure they identify at least two they can use immediately in their own classrooms. Finding appetizers they like isn't a problem. And after hearing how our students respond to these intro-lessons, they're convinced it's worth it to ditch the bland sample set of problems, the pseudo-context examples, and the monotony of a this-is-how-we-always-do-it lesson starters. Excitement in the room soars—until they stumble on that beastly little three-letter word: *but*. Here are a few of the most common concerns we hear from teachers when we talk about appetizers.

"I love what you did with the appetizers and I want to use them in my class, but I don't know if I can afford to give up that much time."

You are totally right! All this new stuff is *just one more thing* to add to an already-packed fifty-five minutes—until it becomes part of your routine. We've had such success building these tasks into the math class, and we think it's not only worth your time to try it in your class—it's worth your time *to read about* trying it in the class. It's *that* powerful.

Let's be clear: We can't afford *not* to spend time engaging our students. If the meat of the lesson is more important than the set-up, it is destined for failure. *Teach Like a PIRATE* describes a lesson without the proper set-up as plopping an uncooked steak in front of a dinner guest: not too appetizing by itself.

If you're concerned about not having enough time for appetizers, we challenge you to note how much time you spend on each aspect of your class day, including all transitions throughout each period. How much time do your students spend on warm-ups? How much time does it take for them to get their pencils and materials out?

The vast majority of these appetizers take less than nine minutes— nine minutes of meaningful conversation, high-quality think-time, and a platform for students to have a voice in a math class. For reference, we were already spending seven-ish minutes on warm-ups before we shifted to appetizers. Adding two minutes to the start of our day was completely worth it, especially when the entrée was much better received. We got back much more than two minutes when the appetizer helped to build a class culture of risk-taking. Students were much more likely to suggest an answer that was way off-base after talking about something that didn't scare them.

To be fair, sometimes the appetizers we love take much longer than a normal warm-up. A prime example: asking students if they would rather have 20 ounces of gold or 1,450 ounces of silver.[1] We could've spent nine minutes on it, but the students demanded more time.

20 ounces of pure gold OR 1,450 ounces of pure silver?

"Yeah, the silver might be more valuable now, but the graph makes it seem like it's gonna get cheaper before the gold."

"I see your point, and this website (the Federal Reserve) says that the market is predicting there will be more gold coming in to bring down the price."

Oh, yeah, let students continue the appetizer.

> **"These appetizers are all wonderful, but my students are hard enough to control as it is. I fear using these will just create chaos."**

---

1 WouldYouRatherMath.com/goldsilver

We've never been in your classroom and won't make a blanket assumption that a quality appetizer is the only solution to a chaotic classroom. Adding a twist to a day might be all it takes to turn chaos into cooperation and mayhem into manageable. Try it out!

Like many of the ideas we share, we're willing to continue taking grand risks. Our students will see our risk-taking, respect it, and be forgiving when a lesson flops. Or—even better—be disappointed when you cut it short because they misbehave.

"It's obvious the students you taught ate this stuff up, but I teach elementary students and those appetizers are too tough for them."

True, we are secondary math teachers. However, it's also very true that we have taken elementary math concepts and ramped them up to meet the needs of our high schoolers. We learn from a lot of great teachers online and elsewhere, no matter what grade level or content area they teach. Because of this, much of the work we do with our students is naturally cross-curricular and scalable to meet the needs of nearly all student ability levels. Good teaching is good teaching, no matter the grade or the subject.

With the "Gold versus Silver: Would You Rather?" task in mind, imagine an elementary discussion about weight, with the teacher doing much of the conversion or giving the conversion factor and turning it into division practice. Imagine a high school economics or social studies discussion about current gold and silver prices and what historical data has shown about pricing of precious metals during critical times in history. Imagine a conversation starter for a middle school earth science class about precious metals and their properties.

During a Classroom Chef workshop for secondary math teachers, we put this assignment onto the screen:

"Write as many expressions as you can that equal eleven."

While a music cue played, some teachers feverishly wrote down the most complex expressions they could possibly imagine. Others, less energetic about flexing their mathematical muscles, opted for the low bar of entry. Fifty-five seconds passed, and a room full of teachers created expressions which total eleven. Once the music ended, John went back to the podium.

John: Okay, folks. Whaddaya got for me?

Sarah: Three factorial plus the square root of twenty-five.

John: Thank you. Next?

Jeff: Five plus six.

John: Thank you. Next?

Damon: Six x minus seven.

John: Thank you. Next?

Diane: Two plus the square root of nine?

John: Thank you. Next?

This continued as Matt dutifully wrote the responses on a piece of chart paper. After the first response, people were *ooh-ing* and *aah-ing*. The second response got nothing. The third got a few chuckles from people who knew the guy who provided it, almost as if they expected it from him.

$$3! + \sqrt{25}$$
$$5 + 6$$
$$6x - 7$$
$$2 + \sqrt{9}$$
$$\log_2 2048$$
$$1 + 5 + 5$$

But with the fourth response, people started to wriggle in their seats because they knew: Two plus the square root of nine is *not* eleven. When they looked to John for acknowledgment of the error and didn't see any, they became even more uncomfortable. Some started mumbling to one another:

"Wait. Two plus radical nine isn't eleven—right?"

"No, it's not. Do you think he realizes that?"

"Pfff. Some 'expert.' Can't even do seventh-grade math."

The remaining expressions equaling eleven were also interesting and eventful, but there is something about those first four that define what happens in a traditional math classroom.

"Now, I want you to reflect back on what happened here," John said, pointing to the expressions on the chart paper. "Sarah gave a rock-solid example and we all got excited. Sarah, that was impressive; I wanted to run over and give you a high five right away. But I didn't; I wanted to give Jeff the same opportunity to tell me five plus six is *also* eleven without feeling stupid for sharing such an apparently simple expression."

John crossed to the front of the room and faced the scattered tables and chairs. "Reflecting on my own career, I spent too much time validating the interesting answers and not enough time validating the *right ones*. Think about this: When Sarah replied with her high-level expression, everyone was impressed, but Jeff (representing the shy student) was likely intimidated to share his answer, *knowing* his expression wouldn't get anywhere close to the positive reaction Sarah's did. When we—the teachers—remove the disparity in how we validate responses, our students benefit."

No longer transcribing expressions, Matt shuffled over and added, "Even though your students may see a number and a prompt, you see this as a prime chance to formatively assess your students. Without their knowing it, through this activity, we have determined who understood yesterday's lesson about square roots. Doing this 'math talk'[2] with our students gives us a glimpse into their heads. While there's nothing wrong with 'five plus six,' it shows me I need to work harder with this student to build enough confidence for him to use the material we're discussing in class. Plus, getting some complex expressions is a lot more exciting."

John smiled, sensing the tension in the room as forty-five math teachers stare at the chart paper. "Now, is there anything on the board that you want to talk about?"

Immediately, four hands shoot up and Matt takes responses from around the room. "Two plus the square root of nine is *not* eleven!" cries a relieved teacher. A few chuckles erupt from around the room as Diane, the teacher who offered the equation, goes red in the face and

---

2 MathTalks.net is loaded with rich conversation starters for a variety of student levels. Created by Fawn Nguyen, this is something that will certainly benefit your classroom.

scoots down in her chair.

Matt asks, "Diane, is there anything we can do to this expression so it *does* equal eleven?"

"Well… yes," she sheepishly replies. "Two plus the square root of nine *plus the square root of thirty-six* should do it. It was a simple error on my part."

That last part.

No matter the color of the pen, when a problem is marked wrong, it defeats many of our students. And we've all done this to our students.

> ## NO MATTER THE COLOR OF THE PEN, WHEN A PROBLEM IS MARKED WRONG, IT DEFEATS MANY OF OUR STUDENTS.

A negative response to incorrect answers cements the idea that going back to correct an error is more foolish than stepping up to admit a mistake.

Diane experienced this feeling. Yes, she made a simple error. We *all* make them. However, giving Diane the opportunity not only to correct the error but also to make it better validated that it was fine to make a mistake, as long as she fixed it. And if she had struggled, she was in a room full of math teachers who were chomping at the bit to help her.

Why did we choose eleven? Simple: May eleventh was the date of the workshop.

Whether done once a week, every third day, or mixed throughout a unit, a "math talk" gives you insight into the true level of your students' mastery of a concept and gives your students a platform on which to use their knowledge and solidify their own success.

When a teacher complains, "These are just too tough for my students!" we hear, "This is more work than I'm willing to do to make it work for my class." Remember, teaching is hard. Creating great learners is even harder. We owe it to our students to constantly seek meaningful ways to engage them and pique their curiosity.

When choosing or creating appetizers for your class, keep in mind that a good appetizer is *frequent, interesting, real,* and *entry-level.*

A Good Appetizer Is Frequent

Once your classroom routine is consistent, adding a regular appetizer to the process takes very little time to prep, and the students adjust quickly.

"Okay, class. Usually, we do table of contents, gluing, then 'Good Things.'[3] Starting today, it's gonna be table of contents, glue, *estimations*, then 'Good Things.' Let's practice now."

Sergio Hernandez, who taught next door to Matt for three years, once said, "Authority is the product of consistency." Your routine must happen consistently so students know how to get the process started. If you're not sure they can do that, ask a teammate to come into your class during their prep period and *ask your students* what they do every day. When they can articulate the routine ("Mr. Vaudrey always has us write down our guesses on this paper. Then we write the answer here and put them back in the folders. Then we talk about 'Good Things.'"), you'll know, even if you have a sub, your appetizer process should run smoothly—whether or not you got the *good* sub.

A Good Appetizer Is Interesting

Many of the appetizers we used in the first parts of our career were bland and seemingly irrelevant to our students, as we previously mentioned. By crafting the introduction of a lesson to immediately engage

---

3 Students can volunteer to share with the class some "Good Things" going on in their lives. If no one volunteers, three students are chosen at random and held "hostage" until they find *something* to be happy about.

our students, whether it is a puzzle, a challenge, or something relevant to the world around them, we are making it easier for them to emotionally and mentally invest in the overall message of the lesson. Oddly enough, we get a lot of mileage out of appetizers dealing with toilet paper.[4] Toilet paper is silly, fun, unusual—and students are *interested* in talking about it. Something we didn't think students would be interested in was the debate between gold and silver prices (from the Would You Rather task). However, the students found it relevant enough to invest in the topic and dig deeper to defend their position.

A GOOD APPETIZER IS REAL

Please hear us: *Real* doesn't mean "students will experience it during their lifetime." But a good appetizer must be something students can understand, grasp, and be something for which they have a frame of reference. Matt's dad describes this connection as mentally "having a shelf to put it on." Robert Kaplinsky calls it "a context to reference throughout the unit." In either case, it's a thing that students can use to build neural connections.

Teaching rational expressions (below) to high school students is tough at first because students don't have a shelf to put it on. They've never seen anything like it and can't see how it applies to them.

The solution isn't to give a contrived example that stretches reality, urging students that rational expressions are used to calculate the number of goals in a game or the height of a flagpole. Pseudo-context like this shows students that math is like vegetables: gross stuff that adults dress up in an attempt to make it attractive to kids.

Instead, imagine a teacher who enters class in workout clothing and declares, "Which one of you mental bodybuilders wants a brain workout? I got one for you. Check this out."

---

4 "How Many Sheets on the Roll of Toilet Paper?", *Estimation 180*, accessed February 24, 2016, http://www.estimation180.com/day-28.html.

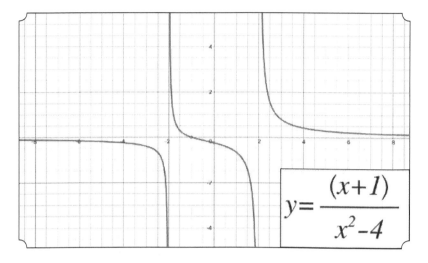

$$y = \frac{(x+1)}{x^2-4}$$

With a simple reframing from the teacher, students view a challenging topic as a brain workout and a puzzle. Then it's a *real* lesson—even though it's quite rare to use rational expressions in real life.

A Good Appetizer Is Entry-Level

All students can discuss toilet paper, gold and silver prices, and paying more for bigger shoes. All students have eaten candy corn (even once), most students have eaten pie, and plenty of students know how the combustion engine works Access is the key to engaging all students with a solid appetizer. If a student has never been to Hawaii or doesn't play guitar, she is locked out of a conversation related to those things.

Yes, appetizers take time. Yes, incorporating them into your routine will require a little practice. And *yes*, they are worth the effort. By starting your class well, you get kids excited about what's in store for the lesson that day. And experts agree: Students who are engaged are easier to manage. If they're bored, they'll find something else to do—and you won't like what they find.

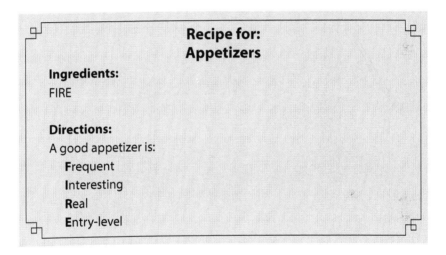

**Recipe for:
Appetizers**

Ingredients:
FIRE

Directions:
A good appetizer is:
    Frequent
    Interesting
    Real
    Entry-level

Entrées

The plate comes around the corner, sizzling like it's still on the grill. This plate is the focus of the meal. In fact, it's the main reason we choose the restaurant. The appetizers, sides, and desserts are nice additions, but they are "support staff" for the entrée—the main dish.

When someone asks what you had at Ferino's, you don't say "garlic bread" or "salad." You say "pizza" or "chicken Parmesan."

And when students ask each other, "What did you do in math today?" the entrée is typically the answer:

"Fractions."

"Graphing."

"Equations."

"I don't know."[1]

Those are okay answers (except for the last one), but in a well-crafted lesson, the students' answers aren't mathematical at all. "What did you do in math today?"

"Mullets."

"Barbie Zipline."

"Earthquakes."

"Big Sharks."

"Billboards."

This is where we might clash with some of the latest educational trends; we would much rather students have a meaningful experience in class than restate a standard. If the lesson was meaningful enough to students that they can recall the theme of the day, that's a step in the right direction.

Here's how it might look.

---

1 A sure sign that the goal of the day wasn't clear and the fifty-five minutes were a waste of everybody's time.

Recipe for:
Memorable Entrée

Ingredients:

1 crazy idea
1 class full of skeptical students
1 gallon of curiosity
Colleagues as desired

Directions:

Mix desired number of colleagues with the crazy idea as needed. Bring the curiosity to a simmer, then quickly combine the crazy idea in a mixing bowl. Introduce to the class of skeptical students and bring to a rolling boil.

CHAPTER 6
BARBIE ZIPLINE

> **From:** Paula Torres <ptorres@cjuhsd.org>
> **Thurs, Apr 2, 2015 at 1:21 PM**
> **To:** John Stevens <jstevens@cjuhsd.org>
>
> Hey John, we've got a couple Fridays at the end of the year that we want to do something fun. How about you come out and do Barbie Zipline for our Integrated II students?
>
> ●━━━━━━━━━━━━━━●
>
> **From:** John Stevens <jstevens@cjuhsd.org>
> **Thurs, Apr 2, 2015 at 1:22 PM**
> **To:** Paula Torres <ptorres@cjuhsd.org>
>
> UMMMM, YESSSS!

Barbie Zipline is a lesson I (John) love for many reasons. One, it takes me out of my comfort zone as a teacher; anything could go wrong here, and that scares me. Two, it confuses the kids. After all, walking into class and seeing a table full of dolls isn't exactly the norm in any math class. Three, it truly is a full-course meal. The appetizer provides a natural transition to the entrée, which seamlessly flows into the dessert, all accompanied by engaging side dishes. Four, it's fun, and I love having fun, especially when it comes to working with an otherwise bland standard—the Distance Formula. The lesson, like all memorable entrées, requires a little preparation, but the results are well worth the effort. My prep for the lesson began with the essential question: **What's the most fun way for Barbie to zipline safely?**

PREPARING THE LESSON: ZIPLINE

Barbie Zipline gets students excited about learning the Distance Formula. You—the teacher—will need to know a few things before the day of the lesson, like the height of the spot where you're going to set up your zipline and send Barbie flying. You'll also need to have a doll (or several so you can divide students into small groups). Aside from that, you'll need a handout.[2] I created one that included an appetizer and gave students a place to show their work. I knew it had to be *good*.

The first rendition of my handout conveyed the message, but it wasn't ready to complement a lesson I had spent so much time preparing. I made small, subtle changes to show the students that I had invested time and effort in this activity. By adding graphics, fine-tuning the input tables, and rewording the questions with simpler prompts, students could see that this lesson was going to be different. And I even printed it on *pink* paper. (The *little* things make the *biggest* differences in the success of a lesson.) One big "Aha!" for me was that the handout had no numbers on it. As Dan Meyer says, this is a case where "the math serves the conversation," and can help us make sense of the world.

One of our favorite side-dish resources (discussed later) is YouTube, and I found the perfect video there for the lesson. If you're still trying to work out the difference between planning and preparing a lesson, think of it this way: Writing a lesson plan means you find the video and you're done. *Preparing* a lesson means you need to make the lesson work from start to finish. As an instructional coach, I also wanted to

---

2 All resources available at classroomchef.com/zipline.

make sure the lesson would work for other teachers with varying levels of comfort with technology and risk-taking. Even though I liked the video I'd found, it was too long and included an inappropriate comment, so I trimmed it down to the good stuff with some basic video editing. Using a video trimmer, I pasted in the link and was able to show my students *only* the part of the video that would pique their interest.[3]

The goal was to have the lesson ride the momentum built by the video without focusing too much on the teacher—tough because the lesson includes a component of direct instruction. And since the class needed appropriate context[4] and multiple teachers would be teaching the lesson for the first time, I even prepared the lesson guide.

GET OUT OF THE VACUUM

No matter how far back you stand from your artwork, it's impossible to escape the vacuum of your own perspective. The same principle holds true for our lessons. To get a different perspective, I sent my lesson preparation to Chris Duran and Paula Torres,[5] the teachers I was working with to bring Barbie Zipline to their school, and asked two questions we don't ask often enough:

What is this missing?

How can it be better?

They were able to point out gaps and make suggestions. Paula suggested adding a couple of videos at the end of the lesson to step it up a level. Chris offered minor tweaks up to the day of the lesson. In addition, I reached out to some great math teachers on the Internet who created a Desmos graph specific to the path of the zipline to make it

---

3   This is a modified version of a video called "Dragon's Breath Zipline in Labadee Haiti," TubeChop video, tubechop.com/watch/7656303.

4   This isn't always the case. If the students had instruction the day before and you're confident they understood it, just dive right into the fun stuff.

5   @chrduran and @Lohstorres1 on Twitter, respectively.

easier to find the length of cord needed. The main takeaway from this: Asking for honest feedback is critical. The input from other teachers raised this lesson from a "B+" to an "A."

SERVING UP A WELL-PREPARED LESSON

Math doesn't have to be bland. In fact, the right prep can make it downright exciting. If you don't want to send students into a "Can I go to the bathroom?" frenzy,[6] you've got to spice up your lessons; make them interesting! For the Barbie Zipline lesson, the opening video relieves some of the dryness of the distance formula.

Based on the students' comments on the day of the lesson, the video did the trick:

"Oh my gaaaaawsh! Are we going ziplining?"

"Holy crap, that looks like fun!"

"Mr. Stevens, ummm, what…what are we doing?!"

After showing the video, I posed the question:

"What would it take to create a successful zipline?"

Cue the mayhem! Kids started shouting—and they weren't shouting nonsense. They were using these weird words like *slope*, *distance*, *angles*, *trajectory*, and *height*. If there was ever a time to let kids get loud, this was it.

Once they calmed down, I pointed out a couple of key components. One, they were actually using academic vocabulary. Two, they were using that vocabulary successfully to describe a high-quality zipline experience.

---

6 We are *not* claiming that engaged students don't need to pee. We *are* claiming that unengaged students ask for bathroom breaks much more often.

Safe Yet Fun

Once students had set the foundation, their focus turned to the details. What kind of zipline would be good? As students gave their answers, I responded—very *literally*—"It needs to have a steep slope." I drew the path of a bungee jumper (sans the bungee) plummeting to their death.

"Nah, you'd have dead customers!"

"You'd actually only have *one* customer because you'd be out of business!"

Then a student called out, "It needs to have a horizontal slope." So, I drew a horizontal line from the platform, extending due east.

"NOOOOO, that would be *boring*!"

"Put it in the middle!"

"We need a slope that would be safe, but fun at the same time."

Gotcha.[7]

With nothing more than a video and a scenario, the students had crafted the framework for what we were going to do. Rather than

---

7   Not all classes got here so quickly. Some required more prompting.

endanger their lives to test their theories, they would use a doll named Tammy. (Adding a name personalizes things. And I wanted the students to take care of Tammy, even though they were already plotting her demise.)

THE MAIN COURSE

Using their handout and newfound knowledge of ziplining, students determined the best distances for Tammy to travel so that she could enjoy a safe, yet fun, zipline. Students quickly identified the height for the start of the line. In this particular school, the start was on top of the math building.

Because it pays to be prepared, I had pre-measured the height and knew it was eighteen feet (this was our standard starting height for the entire class). The students also wanted to know the maximum length they could be from the building.

They knew that they would launch the zipline the following day, but prior to testing the distances with their dolls, students needed to complete the work for at least three different scenarios. Given the starting height and a horizontal distance, each group was to determine how long the zipline cord needed to be.

Example

Starting Height	Horizontal Distance	Zipline
18 ft.	65 ft.	
19 ft.	40 ft.	
18 ft.	90 ft.	

For the first time in a long time, some kids didn't want to leave their math class when the bell rang. In fact, they asked if they could come in early and test their distances before school the next day. One group even planned to do some trials at home.

Because it was a large class (thirty-eight students), the kids had been divided into thirteen groups. And since only one "Tammy" was available, I asked each group to bring in a doll (or action figure, stuffed animal, or extra shoe) for the next day's zipline test. One kid even asked, "Can I bring in a quadcopter to film this? I mean, I don't know how to fly it; my dad does. But can he come in and film it for us?"

I enthusiastically responded, "Of course he can!"

SNAGS AND SUCH

"Trial Run Tuesday" arrived. To combat boredom, each trial was timed and students documented the times of at least ten trials that the class ran. In a class with thirteen groups, this meant at least thirteen trial runs, so I wanted to make sure the students had enough data to compare safe and fun with a speed and with a distance. During prep time, I tested my own zipline using twine and discovered that it bunched up and created knots that kept Tammy from gliding down the line. The solution: thirty-pound fishing line.

The groups set up their ziplines and sent their test subject soaring. The lesson was a huge success. The kids learned the distance formula in a way that made sense to them and they saw that their teachers were willing to try something crazy to make math meaningful to them. Some of my favorite comments of the day:

"He's not joking, right? We're actually going to go outside and do this?"

"We thought you were just hyping this up by saying we'd go outside. We didn't think you were going to follow through with it."

"Wait, are we going to do this for real?"[8]

"But if you don't give the zipline enough distance, Barbie's gonna DIE!"

"Can we use calculus on this?"

"Once the angle of depression goes past forty-five degrees, there's no way it's going to be fun anymore."

And not *one* student asked to use the bathroom.

---

8   How sad is this question? We need to make math *real* more often.

CHAPTER 7
MULLET RATIO

The wind breezed through my (Matt's) freshly shaven sideburns and ruffled the long hair on my neck as my students shuffled to class. *This is gonna be good—even if it goes terribly*, I thought.

Judas Priest's Rob Halford growled, "Breakin' the law, breakin' the law!" from the guitar amp under my foot. I watched from my classroom doorway as the seventh graders stared, a pack of them flocking to their classes nearby. One student told her friend, "We have *that* guy next year."

I alternated between giving them a huge grin and a metal-band scowl, and the whole time, my palms were sweating. Before I left the house that morning, I told my wife, "Even if this goes terribly, I'm so excited for today."[1]

After two verses and a chorus of Judas Priest, my eighth graders trundled into view. Too cool to run to class, they chatted with their friends and danced to the tunes coming from my makeshift jukebox.

---

1 My wife, by the way, made sure that I was serious. "Yes, honey; I really did build a lesson based on a tweet from a guy in Canada and now I'm shaving my head into a decades-old haircut for my lesson tomorrow. Can you take a picture? I want to send it to Timon Piccini, who probably has no clue that this is all his idea."

It wasn't until they reached out to shake my hand at the door that they noticed: Mr. Vaudrey had shaved the top and sides of his head, but left the back long.

"Good morning, Mr. Va—*What did you do to your hair?*" asked Mady, simultaneously horrified and intrigued. Kala, Rian, and John Paul gave similar reactions. Vince grinned shyly.

"Good morning," I said to each. "We're discussing mullets today."[2]

Students continued to filter in—and giggles and chatter filled the room. They stood for the Pledge of Allegiance and then began the warm-up while Rian stamped the previous night's homework.

Generally, I speak very little until after the warm-up and homework check. So at this point, I'd been roaming the class in moderate silence for nine *agonizing* minutes as students whispered to one another, *"What in the world is a mullet?"*

At 8:38 a.m., I began my direct instruction.

WHAT IS A MULLET?
"Business in front and a party in the back."

"As you can see here, a 'mullet' is *business* in the front and a *party* in the back.[3] Which of these two is more Mullety?" I asked with a smirk. Immediately, students began using the terminology I'd introduced, which made me chuckle.

Nathan: Well…the hillbilly[4] has a lot of *party*, but his *business* is pretty short.

Miguel: Ha! He said, "His business is short!"

Mr. Vaudrey (ignoring Miguel): Kala?

Kala: The party and business on the hot guy are, like, the same. It's not really a mullet.

Kelsey: The hillbilly has a little too much party in the back, even though his business is the same as the hot guy.

Susy: I think the hot guy has the better mullet because it's more even.

WHICH ONE IS MORE MULLET-Y?

---

3   Earliest documented use of this phrase is the 2001 film *Joe Dirt*.

4   After first period, I named the two gentlemen myself. Not only did it allow students to describe specific traits of each, but, left with no names (like the image above), my students used *very creative* names which were not at all politically correct. If you thought "hillbilly" was bad, it's a good thing you weren't in my first period.

John Paul: Yeah, his business and party are more proportional.[5]

Then, we started arguing.[6]

Armed with new vocabulary, we tackled the guiding question at the top of each page. Young and old, students with As and students with Ds, "gifted and talented" and general ed students—all of them had an equal right to discuss which of the two haircuts was more Mullety.

A word we haven't used yet in the book is *equity*. When all of the students can access the material at their own comfort level, that's an effective math class. In this case, we were discussing a haircut that was mostly extinct before these kids were born. *Every student has equal access to argue something none of them know about.*

WHICH ONE IS MORE MULLET-Y?

After studying three or four pairs of dudes with bad haircuts,[7] my students began to get frustrated.

---

5 As you may have guessed, this is a Gifted and Talented Education class, full of students who are quick to give the answer they think the teacher wants. The conversations were similar in the other periods, but this conversation is indicative of the general flow.

6 Notice a pattern in this book?

7 The next time we did Mullet Ratio in my class, I scoured the internet for mullets that were non-white, non-dude, or both. Quite a few Jheri Curls could be considered mullets, and many bouffants as well. Special thanks to Deion Sanders, Lionel Richie, and Stevie Nicks.

Mady: Mr. Vaudrey, am I right? Which one is more Mullety?

John Paul: Yeah, isn't there a way we could *rank* them?

While this sounds like a student comment I invented for the book, I assure you, a frustrated thirteen-year-old with glasses *actually* asked me this. His comment earned him a fist bump because, suddenly, *math now served the conversation.*

When students came to class, I told them we were going to discuss mullets. I didn't say:

"We're discussing ratios today."

"We're manipulating fractions today."

"After some direct instruction, we'll move on to guided practice and independent practice."

"I cut my hair to build interest for the lesson—which might be terrible—meaning I may have cut my long, flowing locks for nothing."[8]

While all of those comments were true, revealing them too early would've spoiled the journey. And without the journey, there's no catharsis from resolution.[9] At this point, we'd been comparing mullets for twenty minutes, during which no math was done, no paper was used, and no numbers were seen. Only after we *needed* the math did we bring it in. That's what it means for math to serve the conversation; we're not contriving a ridiculous scenario to "need" a math concept that day.

---

8   For more on that, see *Side Dishes.*

9   Imagine if *Star Wars* had started with Darth Vader barking, "Commander, tear this ship apart until you've found those plans, and bring me the passengers; I want them alive! One of them is my daughter who will be rescued by her future husband and my son, after I kill my mentor and the whole space station blows up! And put my face on some merchandise!"

A key thing to remember when serving an entrée is that *the build-up to the reveal is much more important than the reveal itself.*[10] Introducing the content at just the right time in a discussion is an art form in education, one that's overlooked far too often.

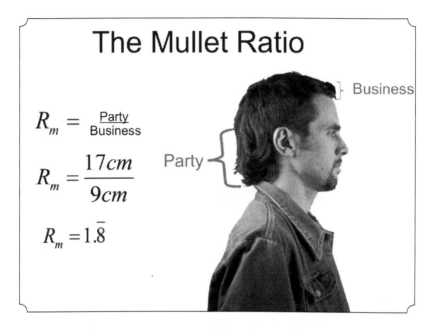

The slide above appeared just in time. If students are frustrated for too long, they begin to lose interest. But this time, they pounced on their calculators like they were tickets to a Jonas Brothers concert.[11] Because they were interested in *mullets*—not proportions. And, let me be clear, so was I. I'd *way* rather discuss *haircuts* than *equivalent fractions.* If we can do both, everybody wins.

---

10 Not just the *prestige* of a magic trick, but the resolution of a problem, as well. (This is also why *Lord of the Rings: The Return of the King* is, like *nineteen* hours long.)

11 It was 2011. The reign of the Bieber was not yet complete.

CHAPTER 8
SCALE FACTOR BILLBOARDS

Staring at the practice problems in the Module Three lesson about scale factor, I (John) felt stuck. I was getting ready to ask my students to turn to page forty-seven in their workbooks and work out problem after problem to learn about taking something small and making it proportionally larger. Could anything be more dry?

Even *typing* the above paragraph was exhausting.

I had two choices: assign the work I was supposed to and run the risk of losing the momentum I had gained by taking "teaching risks" with my students—or go *big* and risk looking stupid if it failed. Clearly, the latter option would have a far greater reward. So I jumped.

Giving kids a *reason* to care about scale factor is the best way to get them to actually care about it. So naturally, I called Bill Houck, general manager of the Southwest division of Lamar Advertising Company. Why? I wanted my kids to work on a billboard design that reflected the morals of our school and showed how we were reaching out to the community. I figured knowing someone from the industry who was coming to speak would make the assignment relevant to them.

Not surprisingly, Mr. Houck agreed to talk to my students about the billboard industry. What was surprising was that he said he would choose one student drawing to display on a billboard in our city for a month. The idea of having their work displayed publicly got almost every kid's interest. Rather than force-feeding them problems in a workbook, the students worked to create a number of designs for Mr. Houck to choose from when he arrived. Then we applied the math, scaling the image up to determine the dimensions needed for display on a real billboard.

A bit of encouragement: Be bold about asking community members to come and speak about their profession. Mr. Houck was an outstanding person for his job at Lamar, but his slow, Louisiana drawl sounded different to California students' ears. And they weren't overly interested in hearing the descriptions of every position in the billboard company. But they loved having him look at the 135 drawings we'd created. He *hmmmed* and *aaaahed*, and then he spotted the drawing he wanted to post on one of his Cathedral City billboards: Efrain's "Helping our Kids Get a View of the Future" design.

Efrain was a quiet but incredibly smart young man who came to my class two months into the year. The "cool" kids liked him because he was smart and knew how to talk the talk. The "smart" kids liked him because he'd acquired enough street cred with the "cool" kids to share his experiences with them.

I'm certain you have an Efrain on your class roster.

News cameras, newspaper journalists, and Efrain's whole family came to see the unveiling of his representation of our school's relationship with community. The drawing itself, which portrays the school's iconic trapezoidal pillars and the city's logo shadowed by the mountains of the valley, may not be relevant to anyone who lives outside Cathedral City, California, but this project will stick with Efrain—and his family—for the rest of his life.

This amazing journey began with my frustration over a scale factor lesson and my decision to pick up the phone. *What was the worst that could've happened?* The GM of the billboard company could've said, "No thanks. I'm too busy," and I would've taught a generic lesson for a day or two. Not the end of the world. Instead, this lesson turned into a semi-annual tradition—something now anticipated by younger siblings of students from my first few years of teaching. One parent even requested me as her son's teacher because of this project.

Yeah, it was that cool.

CHAPTER 9
BIG SHARK

C lass began with some images I (Matt) got from Timon Piccini.[1] Flashing a picture of a megalodon's jaw on the screen instantly captured my students' attention.

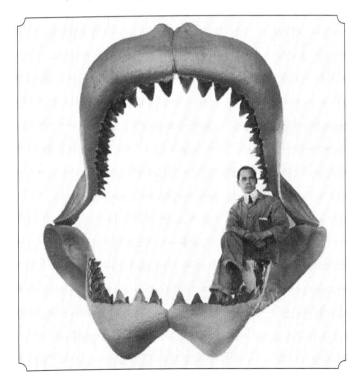

1 Yes, the same guy who planted the seeds for the Mullet Ratio. Maybe he should write a book. Hop on Twitter and tell him so. He's @mrpicc112. More images at MrVaudrey.com/bigshark.

A collective "*Whoaaaaa!*" spread across the room.

Students immediately started asking questions.

Alex: How tall is that guy?

Marie: Is that shark still alive?

Dylan: What's his Mullet Ratio?

Mr. Vaudrey: Aw, you're a sweetheart. What else?

Lorraine: Do any other organisms live in a symbiotic relationship with it?

Mr. Vaudrey: Wow. Ms. Smith[2] owes you a high five for that one. What else?

Alyssa: Is he sitting, like, really far back to make it look bigger?

Luis: What does that shark eat?

Frankie: Is that a megalodon?

To which I responded, "What's a megalodon?"

Frankie had the class's full attention as he stood on his chair and described the giant prehistoric shark large enough to destroy boats and battle a giant octopus. He was crushed to find out that the megalodon is actually extinct and has never been captured on film, despite what the Discovery Channel had him believe.

"But!" I say, borrowing Frankie's excitement and pausing dramatically, "Scientists noticed a lot of similarity between this..." (pictured below).

_____

2 Science teacher on our team at Mountain View Middle School, Moreno Valley, CA. Go Team Awesome!

"and … this" (below).

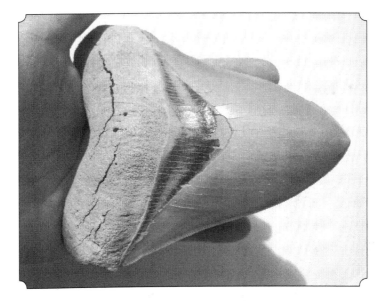

What's happening here? I ask.

Frankie: Are you holding a shark jaw?

Kamiah: Is that a great white shark? Did you catch it?

Mr. Vaudrey: Yes. With my bare hands. And yes, it's from a great white. It's like a smaller version of the megalodon. Do you see the similarities?

We went back and forth between the two pictures as the students nodded.

Mr. Vaudrey: How do you think those two sharks are related?

Tionne: Well, like, what if the megalodon was…like…the ancestor…of the great white?

Luis: No, it's not. This one is way smaller.

Tionne: Yeah, it is! Look at dinosaurs and like…lizards and stuff!

Mr. Vaudrey: You're both right. The megalodon is related to the great white shark, but the great white is way smaller. Does anybody disagree? [I paused for a second and, when there were no dissenters, continued.] Scientists noticed what Tionne noticed—the jaws are similar and the megalodon was probably related to the great white shark we have today. But here's the thing: The skeleton of a shark isn't bone—it's cartilage. So we don't actually *have* a full skeleton of the megalodon, so we don't know how long it was.

The students fell silent, bummed because they wanted to know how big a megalodon was. But they also knew I wouldn't string them along only to leave them unsatisfied.

Mr. Vaudrey: Scientists noticed this, though. What do you notice here?

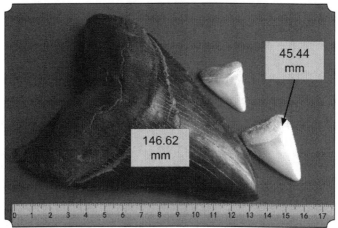

Frankie: What is that?

Deon: Damn! That's a big tooth!

Lorraine: They kinda look the same.

Mr. Vaudrey: Tionne, do you agree?

Tionne: What?

Dylan: Those little ones are the same shape as the big one.

Mr. Vaudrey: Dylan, tell us more about that.

Dylan [after walking up to the board]: This big black one is the same shape as these little white ones.

Mr. Vaudrey: Tionne, do you agree?

Tionne: I think so. Like, they look similar.

Mr. Vaudrey [skipping back to the jaw photos]: Vanessa, what do you notice here?

Vanessa: Those jaws are similar, too. The megalodon jaw looks like a big version of the great white jaw.

Mr. Vaudrey: Everybody nod if you agree. [I paused.] What questions do you still have?

Antonio: How big is the megalodon?

Mr. Vaudrey: Pfff. I don't know. How could we find out?

Dylan: Hang on! [The class was silent, watching Dylan squint at the board.] So, like, if the teeth are ten times as big, then the megalodon is ten times as big.

Mr. Vaudrey: Hmmm…[I paused to let the class think about what he'd said.] Andrew, do you agree?

Andrew: Um…I'm not sure.

Mr. Vaudrey: Ramiro?

Ramiro: Maybe like…*six* times as big. Not ten.

Mr. Vaudrey [skipping back to the image of teeth]: Talk to your neighbor. How much bigger do you think the megalodon is than the great white?

As the "talk to your neighbor" song played, students squinted at the board and held up fingers to "measure" teeth. A few walked up to the board and measured with their rulers, until …

Victor: Ramiro, the numbers are *right there!*

Ramiro: Huh?

Victor: On the tooth in the little gray box!

The song ended and students shuffled back to their seats and got quiet. I asked, "So, what did your group talk about?"

Andrew: Um…we…um…we divided the megalodon tooth and the great white tooth and we got…um…what did we get?

Mr. Vaudrey: Thank you, Andrew. Tricia, siddown. Mia, why did Andrew divide?

Mia: I don't know.

Mr. Vaudrey: I'll come back to you. Ramiro, why did Andrew divide?

Ramiro: Because I told him to.

Mr. Vaudrey: Fine. *Why?*

Ramiro: Because we were trying to find how many *times* as big, so we...like...divided to find it.

Mr. Vaudrey: Mia, why did Andrew divide?

Mia: Because we wanna find out how many times.

Mr. Vaudrey: Tristian, why did Andrew divide?

Tristian: Can I sharpen my pencil?

Mr. Vaudrey: Yes, but first, why did Andrew divide?

Tristian: To...um...figure out how many...like...how many little sharks in the big shark.

Mr. Vaudrey: Close enough. Go sharpen. Dylan?

Dylan: If we compare the teeth, can we figure out the length?[3]

Mr. Vaudrey: Good question! And as luck would have it, we happen to have a place to work that out on page 68! Go there.

Fanda: Wait, how *long* is the great white?

Mr. Vaudrey: Oh, yeah. Here. (See right.)

The students began calculating as I strolled the room, prompting students to check one another's work. Then as a class, we filled in our notebook.

The numbers on the right side of the Essential Question chart were technically correct, but we had spent so long talking about the shark, we needed some redirection. I took a deep breath and declared, "Whoooooooa! The megalodon was between 56.35 and 64.4 feet long!"

Facts About Great White Sharks

Status: Vulnerable

Type: Fish

Diet: Carnivore

Size: 15 ft (4.6 m) to more than 20 ft (6 m)

Weight: 5,000 lbs (2,268 kg) or more

Good to Know: Great white sharks can sense a single drop of blood in 25 gallons (100 liters) of water. They can smell tiny amounts of blood up to 3 miles (5 kilometers) away!

---

3 My intervention classes didn't get to this question as quickly. It took a little nudging and looking at the work on proportions from the previous day. Also, a highly scaffolded page from their notebooks is available at MrVaudrey.com/bigshark.

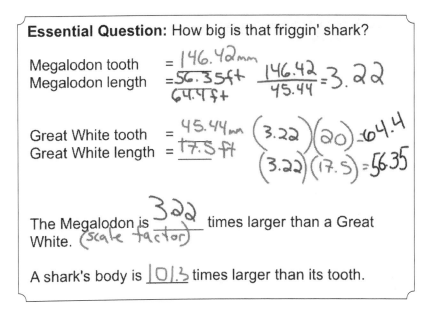

Essential Question: How big is that friggin' shark?

Megalodon tooth = 146.42mm
Megalodon length = 56.35ft $\frac{146.42}{45.44} = 3.22$
64.4ft

Great White tooth = 45.44mm $(3.22)(20) = 64.4$
Great White length = 17.5ft $(3.22)(17.5) = 56.35$

The Megalodon is 3.22 (scale factor) times larger than a Great White.

A shark's body is 10.5 times larger than its tooth.

But the students—with their mushy adolescent brains—stared blankly back at me. They couldn't grasp *abstractly* how long that was in real life.

So we went outside for a *concrete* representation.

From the blacktop, students took twenty "big steps," which varied—much like the size of a shark would have varied—between 56.35 and 64.4 feet, depending on the length of their strides.

Mr. Vaudrey: Everybody turn around and look back at the blacktop. The distance from you to the blacktop is the about length of a megalodon.

From the back of the crowd, Alan exclaimed, "Holy shit! That's a big shark!"

Back inside, I showed them this picture.

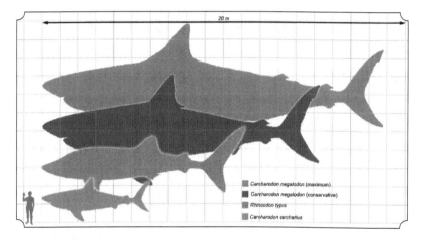

Maria: I wonder how tall the fin is.

Fernando: Could the big shark swallow a bus?

Ramiro: How many humans could it eat at once?

Mr. Vaudrey: Let's get into those questions tomorrow.

Nobody in my department was concerned I spent an extra day or two on proportions. And nobody in the office minded that we went outside and walked around for a little bit. Even if they had cared, it was worth it; every student built some connections between sharks and math and proportions. For the class, math was meaningful.

CHAPTER 10
SEPTEMBER 11TH

BEEEEEP. BEEEEEP. BEEEEEP. Whap!

The alarm that sounded through my gym-locker-scented dorm room at Taft College meant I (John) needed to hurry to my 7:45 a.m. class. After all, my baseball coach was my professor; I couldn't be late to his class. My dorm mates and I had returned from a fall baseball trip the night before, and the four-hour bus ride had gotten to us—so naturally, we started a food fight. We'd flung food **everywhere**. Knowing we would be running for hours if Coach found out, we'd cleaned up the oranges and spare parts of sandwiches, but the still-fresh memory made me smile as I headed to class, stepping over some orange splatter and a sandwich wrapper that were overlooked by our cleaning efforts. Oh well, I thought, I'll get it after class. Before I got out my door, Manny Rodriguez, the non-stop laughing underclassman everyone loved, yelled, "Hey, Stevens, we're going to war!"

"C'mon man, we can't. Coach is already going to be ticked when he finds out about this. Last night was fun, but we gotta stop. I need to get to class."

*"No, I don't mean food war. Get in here. We're going to **war**."*

The second plane hit the South Tower just as I stepped into his room. Our lives haven't been the same since.

During my first year in the classroom, I asked students about 9/11. Dumbfounded, they asked, "Why would this matter to us?"

I was taken aback. "What do you mean, why would this matter to you?! This is a part of our history! We all know where we were that day, at that time. Wait—you were only eight years old. Hold up. We need to talk."

DISCLAIMER: *This is from my second year teaching. There are faults. This is before I was blessed with the know-how to let students run wild with technology. This was before the fads and trends of EdTech started, at least for me. This is before the iPad existed. This was what I knew to be the best way to teach at the time. I've made changes to the lesson preparation since this story, but the premise of creating a meaningful experience remains.*

The opening story above was the hook for my students on September 11, 2007. The students knew something was up when I started class by talking; usually I played a video, showed them a picture, or gave them a problem to solve. With my story that day, I wanted them to feel even the slightest bit of emotion I did on 9/11—and still feel, even fifteen years later. They were floored. The room was the quietest it had been during the first two weeks of the school year—probably quieter than it was the rest of the year. My story—the appetizer—pulled them in. The videos we watched next of the 9/11 media coverage had them completely hooked.

I then handed the students a worksheet and told them to work in pairs to find the answers. It may seem like I was trying to weasel some math into a history lesson—or some history into a math lesson.

Regardless, it worked. Emotions stoked the conversations that came as they discovered the answers to the questions on the handout.

Because the students had no memory—no context—of what happened on September 11, 2001, I had to create it. By unfortunate coincidence, the number of people who died on 9/11 was comparable to the enrollment of the neighboring high school that most of the students would attend the following year. Many of them had friends or family currently attending there.

"Imagine if one day, everyone at Cathedral City High School was gone. Gone. That's what those families still live with to this day."

Silence. The success of this lesson hinged on my students' desire to know more. If there was going to be a lasting effect, I needed an "It"— that thing your students can't stop thinking about, talking about, or

---

MY STORY, THE APPETIZER, PULLED THEM IN. THE VIDEOS WE WATCHED NEXT OF THE 9/11 MEDIA COVERAGE HAD THEM COMPLETELY HOOKED.

---

feeling. "It" plays with students' emotions. "It" has students engulfed in the moment. The "It" for this lesson was an all-or-nothing attempt to get them to live in the moment of September 11, 2001. It was working.

Some kids got teary-eyed at the tribute video we watched next. I did. Still do. What I wasn't prepared for was Jose, the tough guy who hadn't figured out yet how tough he needed to act to secure his reputation. Jose kept pinching his fresh, white Stafford t-shirt to his eyes, looking up in-between pinches to reveal ever-reddening eyes, but not wanting to miss another picture, another moment.

After the videos and the pictures, questions came pouring in, each one indicating emotion and desire to learn more—to feel more. They asked if they could look up more videos. I agreed, as long as they understood there are tons of completely unsubstantiated conspiracy theories. Yes. Do it. *It was working.*

Two nights before this lesson, as it so often happens in my scattered brain, a thousand ideas, thoughts, and memories flooded my path to REM sleep status. One idea woke me so I could write it down: *Talk to Lowe's, giant scale model, Twin Towers.*

The next morning during my prep time, I called the local Lowe's hardware store. I explained my idea to the manager, who was more than happy to help. "Sure," he replied. "We can take care of you!"

After school, I picked up enough plywood, two-by-fours, screws, wood glue, and electrical tape for our goal: recreate a 1:100 scale model of the Twin Towers. The students' task was to ask their parents for aluminum foil. Over the course of two weeks following September 11, 2007, we worked together to build those towers. I only did what I was legally required—or completely afraid of handing over to the kids—to do: cut and drill. They measured every cut. They held every piece. They carried out and organized the entire event. They checked for accuracy. They split electrical tape in half and wrapped it around the towers to represent every floor of Tower One and Tower Two. They came in for hours each day after school to work on the towers. *It worked!*

At the end of the project, we stood back and admired what we had accomplished. A group of about twenty eighth graders, in their second, third, and fourth weeks of school, engaged in something I hope they'll never forget.

I believe teachers, by nature, are humble people. We don't seek praise or external affirmation. However, seeing the work these kids did made me realize it would be selfish to let their efforts end there. The general public *needed* to see this. Being the careless second-year teacher I was, I called the district's public relations manager and told her about the project as it was winding down. She sent out a local newspaper and TV reporters to interview us. You can believe the kids were *thrilled* when the news reporter and camera crew walked into our school.[1] *It worked.*

1 The reporter said some nice things about me on the newscast, but that's not why I'm sharing about it. Sure, I'm proud of my students and the work they did. And, yes, it felt great to hear some kudos from the press. But wouldn't it be nice if more teachers were spotlighted in the media for working hard? I think so.

To cap it off, we displayed the towers in the school's multipurpose room for a few weeks where the students' peers could see them.

Yes, this project required a ton of effort. It was also the best lesson I ever taught.[2] We did similar projects every year after, but none as large in scale or time commitment as the Twin Towers built by my students in 2007. My goal was for them to walk away with compassion for the families of those who died and to get an idea of the void that the vacancy of those towers left. The lesson worked; I know I achieved those goals.

All resources mentioned above are available, for free, on our website.[3]

Throughout this project and most of the outlandish projects we've tried with our students, we hope to use mathematics as the plate to support a bigger conversation, a bigger question, and a deeper meaning. By exposing eighth graders to the travesty of 9/11, I hope they now walk with empathy for those involved, even to this day. Sure, the math will fade and the proportional reasoning will diminish, but they will never forget those towers and the lives lost on that day.

As teachers, we have a unique opportunity to affect positive change in ways very few professions can claim. Our customers—the students—are impressionable, emotional, and eager to learn. Each of the examples we have brought forth reach across content areas, grade levels, and dig into the true meat of a meaningful educational experience. Long before they assimilate into the working world, our students can begin to ask tough questions about tough issues and form understandings of complex topics.

---

2 Up to that point.

3 classroomchef.com/911lesson

What purpose does education serve, if not to prepare our students?

While we will discuss taking risks later, now is a great time to mention that all lessons we've done with our kids have come with an inherent risk of failure. Why not go big and get students to question their social impact while we're at it? Why not empower students to stand up, use their voice, and be heard in their community? When we do that, we begin the transition from traditional teacher to Classroom Chef.

However, without asking the right questions and proper plating, our lessons are bound to falter.

Chapter 11
The Plating—Presentation Is Everything!

Jamie Duncan is a first-grade teacher who, by her own admission, didn't try to make math spectacular early in her career. "It's no surprise that my poor mathematical upbringing had an impact on how I taught math in the classroom."

I (Matt) winced when I heard that. How often do we teach the way *we* were taught? Jamie pinpointed the issue for thousands of teachers; students carry bad learning experiences with them for a lifetime.

It was only after attending math workshops that Jamie's perspective was turned on its head and she became curious. Two separate math

How Often Do We Teach the Way We Were Taught?

professionals challenged her by saying that the old direct instruction model was backwards. She was, at first, skeptical, "I went to college. I got my bachelor's and master's degrees, took more classes after that, and somehow *my kids* are better teachers than *I* am? My students learn better when I hardly say anything *at all?* How are they supposed to figure out how to do this math without me instructing them?" she wondered. Jamie noticed two things: her students retained the information better when they *discovered* it, and crafting an environment where students discover the information is really tough at first.

After a while, though, it looks pretty cool.

Cookies and Missing Addends

"Good morning, boys and girls!" Jamie welcomes each student as they hang up their backpack, move their name to the "Buying Lunch" or "Brought Lunch" section of the lunch chart, and get settled for a Friday in Jamie Duncan's first-grade class.

"Come to the carpet, please! I have a question for you."

Jamie's department struggles year after year to teach missing addends to their seven-year-old students. Developmentally, it's a bit of a jump to go from problem A to problem B (below):

$$A.\ 13 + 4 = \boxed{}$$
$$B.\ 9 + \boxed{} = 21$$

The same is true for subtraction; kids struggle with problems like these:

$$A.\ 11 - 8 = \boxed{}$$
$$B.\ 9 - \boxed{} = 4$$

After wrestling with the topic in grade-level meetings, Jamie found a lesson in a blog she was reading, written by an elementary school teacher across the country.

Ain't the Internet great?

"Class, my home was invaded by a monster last night, and look what it did!" Immediately the students' eyes went wide and they began whispering to one another. "A monster? Do you think she saw it? It wasn't a *real* monster; she's just pretending."

Mrs. Duncan then played a one-minute video[1] of the monster's fuzzy hand grabbing a box of cookies off the counter and pulling it out of sight. After some crunching and chewing noises, the monster hand pushes a half-empty box of cookies back into the frame and the video ends.

"What do you notice?" Mrs. Duncan asks the class. The flood of first-grade answers is adorable.

"It's got a fuzzy white hand."

"That's not a *real* monster."

"It ate a bunch of cookies."

"But then it put the box back. Maybe it's a nice monster."

"I like Oreo cookies."

"Now you don't have a full box no more."

As the students offer information, Mrs. Duncan records the students' observations on the whiteboard and writes their names in parentheses after their comment. This practice helps students feel valued in the learning process. All students can contribute.

After the initial burst dies down a bit, she says, "Yeah, I noticed some of those things, too. What do you *wonder*? Head back to your tables and talk to your elbow partner."

In huddled pairs, students jabber excitedly about monsters and cookies. Every student in the class can access the discussion, and Mrs. Duncan has eight students with special needs in her room.

After a couple minutes, Mrs. Duncan calls, "Hocus pocus!"

The students respond back, "Time to focus."

"Hands in your lap."

"And give a clap." Twenty-eight students *clap* their hands together

---

1   It's better if you watch the video yourself: gfletchy.com/the-cookie-monster.

and fold them into their lap.

Mrs. Duncan paces between pods of tiny desks and asks, "What are some things you wonder?" She calls on a few students and writes their questions on the board.

"How big is the monster?"

"How many cookies did it eat?"

"Is the monster full or is it gonna eat more cookies?"

"How many bags of cookies does Mrs. Duncan buy?"

Mrs. Duncan points to each student silently and nods as they share their questions. "Wow, what curious students we have today. I'm curious, too. I heard some students wondering *how many*. Put a thumbs up if your table is also wondering *how many*.

About two-thirds of the class gives a tiny thumbs up.

"Turn to your table," Mrs. Duncan lowered her voice, "and share a *brave estimate* with your group. Go."

Lowering her voice added an air of mystery. Tiny bodies hunched over tables and whispered emphatically to each other, and Mrs. Duncan's students were now giving their brave estimates with conviction and intensity.

"Okay, go to your tools and solve. How many cookies did the monster eat? Go."

Around the room, students lunge for rulers, whiteboards, and counters to show their work. In pairs and individually, students begin drawing cookies, boxes, and numbers. After a few minutes, the chatter subsides and a few students begin scratching their heads.

"What's up, friends?" asks Mrs. Duncan. "It looks like you're getting stuck."

"I can't figure it out."

"We need more information."

Mrs. Duncan smiles. "Okay. Maybe we can find some. What information do you need?"

A plucky girl raises her hand, "I need to know how many cookies are left after he eats them."

Mrs. Duncan flicks her finger across the iPad and this picture appears on the screen.

While students begin counting in the air, a few walk up to the screen and begin counting. This is a key moment; Mrs. Duncan hasn't told the class, "There are twenty-six cookies." She didn't flip to the back of a textbook to show the answer key. She showed a picture and let them work on it.

"Wait!" calls a boy by the screen. "How many cookies came in the box?"

"I dunno," shrugs Mrs. Duncan. "Here."

In math classes across the country, teachers are dishing out work to their students, who receive it with a sigh and grudgingly begin the tedious calculations. However, Mrs. Duncan's class tackles this new information voraciously, and two students yell out at the same time, "Forty-eight!"

Mrs. Duncan raises her eyebrows. "Wow. Does anybody want to revise their estimates?"

"I do!" calls Jeremy.

"Why's that?"

"I thought that the monster ate about ten cookies, but I think he ate more than ten now."

"Thank you, return to your seats. Class, you now have some more information. What do we know? Mariah?"

"We know that there are forty-eight cookies in the package." Mrs. Duncan writes that on the board and asks, "What else do we know? JP?"

"We know that after he ate some cookies, there were twenty-six left."

Mrs. Duncan finishes writing JP's comment and asks, "What do we *not* know yet?"

Rubee raises her hand, "We don't know how many cookies the monster ate."

Mrs. Duncan caps the marker. "Thank you, Rubee. At your desks, figure out how many the cookie monster ate."

The students again work in pairs or individually, drawing, shaping, and modeling. Mrs. Duncan's class has access to math tools all the time. Math buckets and math binders are full of Unifix cubes, base-ten blocks, counters, balance scales, 120 charts, age-appropriate number lines, part-part-whole mats, tape diagrams—you name it. Some chat to each other and others work intently on their own.

At about that time, Mrs. Duncan calls out, "Around the world! Find a friend's desk to sit in!"

At once, all the students rise and circulate through the other pods of desks. Once all students are seated, Mrs. Duncan says, "Think silently to yourself about what your friend did." After a minute of silent *think time*, they discuss the work in front of them with their new table group.

"My person said forty-eight minus something is twenty-six."

"The monster ate at least ten cookies."

"My person said that, too."

"Something minus twenty-six is forty-eight."

"Twenty-six plus something is forty-eight."

And so it proceeds around the room. Students critique each other's work, suggest changes, mark smileys or question marks on the parts they like or the parts that confused them. After plenty of discussion, the students return to their seats and modify their own work to reflect what their classmates said.

After mooching work from someone else in the class, students speak louder and more confidently about the math at their table. Some have stacked tiles to show their thinking, others have drawn cookies (but at some point abandoned drawing forty-eight cookies), and some have used numbers. All are accessing the prompt in a way that's meaningful to them, but they must have a variety of models in order to discuss it with the class.

As students revise at their table, Mrs. Duncan gathers pictures of student work on the iPad, specifically looking for three types of work: *concrete* (counters or base ten blocks), *representational* (drawings, 120 charts, number lines), and *abstract* (equations and numbers). She then projects the images in that order and has a class conversation about them, like this:

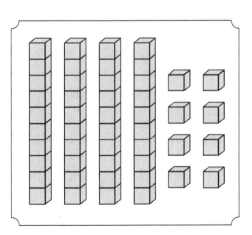

Once students were settled on the carpet, Mrs. Duncan shows them this image and asks, "Why did the student arrange the blocks like this? How many blocks is this? Why did that student choose forty-eight? Is it their favorite number?" The students respond, "That's the number of cookies we started with."[2]

120 Chart

1	2	3	4	5	6	7	8	9	10
11	12	13	14	15	16	17	18	19	20
21	22	23	24	25	26	27	28	29	30
31	32	33	34	35	36	37	38	39	40
41	42	43	44	45	46	47	48	49	50
51	52	53	54	55	56	57	58	59	60
61	62	63	64	65	66	67	68	69	70
71	72	73	74	75	76	77	78	79	80
81	82	83	84	85	86	87	88	89	90
91	92	93	94	95	96	97	98	99	100
101	102	103	104	105	106	107	108	109	110
111	112	113	114	115	116	117	118	119	120

"I can see that this student chose forty-eight and they also chose twenty-six. Jennifer, what did this student do here?"

The students take a few seconds to think about it, but Mrs. Duncan patiently waits, though the ten seconds of silence feels like an eternity. At this point in the year, the students are much better at handling silent think time. So is the teacher.

---

2 Mrs. Duncan later pointed out that students are reasoning abstractly and quantitatively, which is the Standard for Mathematical Practice #2.

Jennifer says, "They counted backwards from forty-eight to twenty-six."

"Andreya, how is that different from what the first student did?" Mrs. Duncan now has both images projected side-by-side.

"Umm...the first picture has forty-eight blocks and took away some. The second picture has counting."

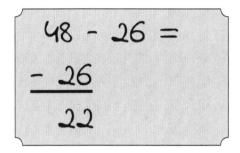

"Mariela, what's happening here?"[3]

Drawing on what other students have said, Mariela pipes up, "She started with forty-eight blocks and took away twenty-six blocks."

"Thank you. Mariela said *blocks*. What else could she have said?"

"Numbers!" "Cookies!" "Blocks!" "Fingers!"

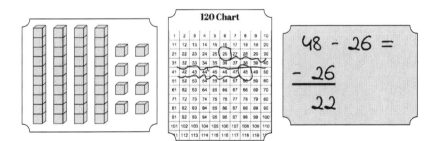

"Talk to your neighbor. How are these three pictures the same, and how are they different?"

---

3   Obviously, these are recreated. For images of sweet student work, head to Jamie's blog: ElementaryMathAddict.com.

After the students chatter for a bit, Mrs. Duncan gets their attention again and *finally* gets to the big question: "Share with your neighbor, how many cookies did the monster eat?"

This time, the chatter is more pronounced and louder, but shorter. It naturally gets quiet and students return their focus to Mrs. Duncan, who patiently sits with a smile. "Would you like to see how many cookies the monster ate?"

The class shouts back, "Yes!"[4]

GOOD QUESTIONS

The difference between a great math lesson and a great math teacher is the questions. A great math teacher can ask questions that get students interested in any lesson, much like a chef can transform even a grilled cheese sandwich into a Mediterranean pesto panini.

Student responses will be all over the map (at first). And they may take some coaxing to navigate toward mathematical thinking and reasoning. One of our jobs is to teach students how to think critically, ask for more information, and identify what's important. They need our patience and guidance as they practice their critical thinking skills,

---

4   We mentioned in *Entrées* that the build-up is more important than the reveal. If you spend an hour talking about something, your reveal had better deliver.

especially early in the year. As math teachers, we must train our students to use skills like these. Memorized formulas are easily forgotten, but skills will stick with our kids for years to come.

Go back through the *Entrée* stories you just read, and look specifically at the questions each teacher asked the students. Notice how no teacher was in a hurry; they let students discuss a topic or an idea until they were satisfied that the students fully understood it.

We have two pieces of good news about student questioning: you can start tomorrow honing those skills, and your class culture will naturally become more accommodating. The process of teacher growth can start right away.

THE PROCESS OF TEACHER GROWTH CAN START RIGHT AWAY.

JAMIE DUNCAN SHARES HER PROCESS

Honestly, if I can make this change, so can everybody else. You just have to be committed. I'm not the best teacher in the world, nor in the state, nor in my county, and not even in my district. I just made a commitment to learn, to be better, and I'm following through.

I used to try to make math easier for my students so they wouldn't have to feel the way I felt about math as a child and adolescent. I always modeled the "best" way to solve a problem using tools that I knew made sense. Students mimicked what I did, whether it made sense to them or not.[5] I was trying to protect them from struggling, but I was sheltering them from the actual learning process itself, which created a repetitive cycle that I was not aware of until now.

I wondered why my students did better when I let them struggle and become the experts of the class. Then it hit me. It was something Ryan Dent and Kristian Quiocho[6] shared at our Standards or Mathematical Practice (SMP) training, though perhaps I wasn't quite ready to fully understand it yet. It was problem-solving. My kids can solve problems, but what *is* problem-solving? Simply put, it is what you do when you don't know what to do. I was creating environments where students were encouraged to use their reasoning and problem-solving skills, and it translated to more meaningful learning.

---

5   Ouch. Been there.

6   You can find these fine educators on Twitter: @4ryandent and @KristianQuiocho.

So I gave students tasks. I watched them struggle (*without* rescuing them; it was excruciating at first!). Students explained their work and critiqued the work of others. They made connections, they talked to each other about math, and they wrote about math in their math journals.

Some of the typical questions I ask kids when they are finishing up their work are, "Does it make sense? If someone else sits down and looks at your work, will they be able to understand it? Did you go back into the context? Where is the proof? Can you show your thinking another way? What equation could you write that would represent your work?" In the lesson above, my standard was "looking for students to use knowledge of base ten and the relationship between addition and subtraction," but the students didn't see that as the focus.

It's so crazy to think of how my math instruction has done a 180. I presented a workshop at CMC called "Primary Students in Powerful Mathematical Discussions...For Real?" and I'll repeat it at NCTM.[7] That simply wouldn't have happened a few years ago.

---

7 California Mathematics Council (South) and National Council of Teachers of Mathematics.

CHAPTER 12
HOW TO MAKE
YOUR OWN ENTRÉE

FOR US, LEARNING TO PREPARE
MEANINGFUL LESSONS IS AS MUCH ABOUT
ENGAGING OUR STUDENTS AS IT IS A
WAY TO PRESERVE OUR SANITY.

For us, learning to prepare meaningful lessons is as much about engaging our students as it is a way to preserve our sanity. We are willing to embrace the messy process of learning ways that make school—and math in particular—relevant to our students. We also know that teaching this way means we have to take grand risks that carry a high potential for failure. Thankfully, with the popularity of online education networks on Twitter, we have realized there are other teachers who are just as outlandish, ambitious, and rambunctious as us. With the support of that kind of community and access to blogs, tools, and books like this one, creating fun lessons is easier than ever.

START WITH THE WORST LESSON

Oh, *excuse* us. You got into teaching because you love *every page* of your textbook and want to share your joy with the world?

For the rest of us, there's at least one lesson we dread every year. For Matt, it's percent mixture problems. If you've ever taught algebra, reading those three words likely made you shiver, groan, and sigh—maybe even gag.

For the uninitiated, they look like this:

A chemist needs 10L of 35% solution. The company shipped 10% solution and 50% solution. How many liters of each solution should the chemist mix to make 35% solution?[1]

Percent mixture problems are a true challenge to teach in a meaningful way, and no part of them is relevant to an eighth grader. Every time this unit rolls around, the math department dies inside a little bit.

Here's the thing: If percent mixture problems were the anomaly, distaste of math class wouldn't be so socially accepted.

But they're not.

By the time students graduate high school, they have seen dozens of chapters with problems just like percent mixture problems which do not get them excited. Then they graduate, have kids of their own, and the disconnect between math and real life leads them to tell their kids, "I'm not a math person."[2] The attitude of *I'm not a math person* is far worse than the attitude *I struggle in math*. The latter is an admission of a current challenge, one that can be beaten with hard work, while the former implies some are born with a math muscle and some are not. This attitude is corrosive to our students, our own work ethic, and our society as a whole.

---

1 3.75 L of the 10% solution and 6.25 L of the 50% solution, and no one cares. Least of all you, the reader. We don't even care, and we're writing the book! These problems truly are the worst. We're sorry we put you through that.

2 For how this statement makes us feel, visit classroomchef.com/gaahh. If you've ever said it, you're forgiven—as long as you never say it again. John will give you infinite high fives if you never say it again.

Truly, many lessons within our required texts are blander than cold, sodium-free chicken broth. Everyone has a lesson, a chapter, or an entire unit in the year-long curriculum which could use a little educational cayenne pepper. You know that lesson—or unit—is coming, and you start stressing out a month in advance, wondering how you're going to make a group of kids think it's worth their time. It's the one you scour the Internet for in search of a really cute worksheet that might mask the really horrible task.

Yeah, sure. That'll fix it.

However, your frustration may not be as blatant or as obvious. For John, it was frustrating to know his students didn't see the value in remembering what happened on September 11, 2001. He was also frustrated to see so many kids doing great work in the classroom but—before the dawn of social media—having nowhere to share it.

For Matt, the textbook's introduction to the scale factor was so awful, the megalodon lesson was a welcome change.

So we're not saying you need to save your best for the worst. We're saying use your best when you know your students need it.

USE YOUR BEST WHEN YOU KNOW YOUR STUDENTS NEED IT.

Figuring out why a lesson frustrates you is a big component of making it better. Is it the lesson's dry discourse? Or maybe a canned assessment which returns no real value to the students, the parents, or you as the teacher? Is it something the students have already seen—year after year after year?[3] Or perhaps it's that fact that, though you're a content expert and have taught the lesson so many times—always the same way—you never see the results you want?

---

3   Yes, we're lookin' at you, improper fractions.

Think back to the Sun Tzu quote about preparing for battle. By going into class first and then seeking to teach, we are setting ourselves up for abysmal failure. It's comparable to seeing someone else's rock-solid lesson, stealing her handout, and thinking you could wing it with your classes.[4] Or, if you prefer the war metaphor, emailing the president with advice on the Middle East because you watched *The West Wing* on Netflix.

When a frustrating element of your curriculum drives you to change it, you must invest the time necessary to prepare the kitchen and set the table. If you want to make the frustrating element less frustrating, be willing to do whatever it takes.

EASE THE SUFFERING

Our best entrées never start with the goal of being one of the best lessons we've ever taught. Instead, they are the by-product of an attempt to make a textbook, module, packet, or even last year's self-created lesson a little less painful and to give it some sort of meaning.

While many curriculum developers use real-world contexts to illustrate math, the team at Mathalicious has the inverse approach: They develop lessons in which students use math to better understand the real world. Lessons explore such questions as whether Olympic sprinter Usain Bolt has an unfair height advantage (proportions), how long it will take people on minimum wage to pay off speeding fines (solving linear functions), and whether video game consoles will ever become fully life-like (exponential growth). Just as a master chef uses a full cabinet of exquisite spices, Mathalicious approaches mathematics as a powerful tool for adding flavor to everything from sports to healthy eating, politics to social justice. For generations, students have asked of

---

4 This has happened. Foolishly, and unfortunately, too many times during our first few years of teaching, we would find a great idea, see it in action, and think we had the chops to roll it right into our lesson plans. How many Bobby Flay recipes have you desecrated in your kitchen at home? Our apologies to you, rosemary flatbread.

math, "When will I ever use this?" Mathalicious lessons help teachers answer that, while creating a classroom culture of conversation, collaboration, and critical thinking.[5] It isn't easy to generate authentic math tasks that intertwine with bigger social implications, but they're doing it better than any company we've seen to date.

As a Classroom Chef, we encourage you to take a similar approach to your mathematical kitchen. Your students don't need to see the recipe card; they need to be interested in the meal. Immerse them in a kitchen of opportunity, conversation, collaboration, and critical thinking, and watch how they respond. Our students are far better prepared to make decisions than we think they are.

Too often, educators are guilty of wrapping math around "real-life" scenarios, and infusing that pseudo-context into lessons. Students can sniff out that garbage the moment it hits the table. It's like molding tofu into a steak shape. You just can't fool them.[6] We want so desperately for our students to find meaning in what we're teaching, we forget how easily our audience can sense foul play.

In order to improve the lesson, chapter, or unit, there needs to be a *boom*. However, not every *boom* is a satisfactory answer to, "When am I ever going to use this in real life?" In fact, real-life relevancy can't

WHEN IMPROVING A LESSON, AIM FOR RELEVANT AND SETTLE FOR INTERESTING.

be the goal because "real life" to thirty-five plus students in your classroom is arbitrary and absurd. Rather than pursuing that monster, we

---

5   Have we mentioned how we love Mathalicious? We have? Well…we'll say it again.

6   Both of us have been guilty of such nonsense. Many times, in fact. It's going to happen. But if we can limit the pseudo-context in lessons, they naturally become more authentic. Also, vegans: No disrespect with the steak thing, but you are *really* missing out.

suggest this: When improving a lesson, aim for relevant and settle for interesting.

To this day, we have both failed to find ways to teach how exponent rules are "real-life" relevant to a group of middle schoolers. Try as we may, for some odd reason, they just don't care that the Richter scale applies the use of logarithms and their coinciding rules. At some point in their life, they might, but now is not the time. And zero kids have perked up when we use stoichiometry from their futuristic chemistry class to show the value of knowing the quotient rule of exponents. Not only is there no "boom," a worksheet about the Richter scale does nothing to make me hungry for exponent rules. And a stoichiometry handout? Completely off-base for middle school—the math involved is far beyond what an eighth grader should ever have to see.

Yep, our appetites are about gone.

Rather than drowning in pseudo-context, maybe the lesson could start with an error analysis of exponent rules, à la Andrew Stadel, as if to say, "Let's call a spade a spade here. Exponents are tough, and they can be even tougher to teach well. Our job today is to make them easier to manage. We're going to pick apart other people's work and figure out where they went wrong." In handing over the ownership of the mistake to someone else, you empower the students to find the faults and correct them. Once again, *boom!*

Ask Your Students for Feedback during and after the Lesson

Think about what a restaurant server does after your food is delivered. Good ones know when to come by your table to ask how everything tastes, whether you need more to drink, and if you need anything else. Then they let you continue enjoying your experience. Awful servers drop off your plate, chat with the bartender until it's clear you're done eating, and then swing by your table with the bill and a smile on their face.

We've all had both types of servers and understand how those experiences shape our entire perception of the meal.[7] We suggest taking an alternate approach in the classroom: Ask your students for lesson feedback. Students will naturally buy into a classroom culture when they feel like their voices matter, and these questions can help involve student voice:

- Is this working?

- What can we do better tomorrow?

- What did we like about the lesson?

- If there was one component to keep from this lesson, what would it be?

- If we could change something in the lesson, what would it be?

- Where could we have done better?

Notice that these aren't "I" questions; they are "we" questions. The responsibility for the tone of the classroom falls on the teacher. When students see you value the process of teaching, they will begin to value—and take responsibility for—the process of learning. The class

> **WHEN STUDENTS SEE YOU VALUE THE PROCESS OF TEACHING, THEY WILL BEGIN TO VALUE AND TAKE RESPONSIBILITY FOR THE PROCESS OF LEARNING.**

culture, then, is the responsibility of *all*, but it begins with you involving your students in the process of creating a better learning experience.

When we take a lesson to the staff lounge or lunchroom and ask our

---

7   Also, if you ate at the Pizza Hut in West Dundee, Illinois, in 2002, Matt apologizes; he was an awful server.

peers to make it better, they're seeing the lesson through a teacher's lens. Naturally, our fellow teachers will consider what we say, offer a couple tweaks, and we take the lesson back to class the next period (or next day or week) and give it another go. But any changes are made based on a teacher's perception of the lesson.

When we ask our students about the lesson, we get multiple vantage points on the effectiveness of the message and an array of ideas about how to make it better. Of course, we also open ourselves to their criticism of our pedagogy and practice, but we can *improve* through criticism. In fact, this is really the only way we can find out how to better serve our students. We must listen to our students' point of view and use our professional judgment to determine what will work best. Creating a class culture where it is acceptable to appropriately criticize work is difficult, but necessary, for the growth we seek in our classrooms. Also, as you'll read in the *Desserts* section, when students are involved in this way and begin to take responsibility for their role in the class culture, they are much more forgiving when a lesson doesn't go as you'd hoped.

Find Someone Who Can Make It Even Better

We get it. Your lesson is infinitely better than it was yesterday. But truth be told, it could still improve (no hard feelings). As we've said before, while we are definitely our own worst critics, that doesn't make us our own best critics.[8] Each of us is harder on ourselves than anyone will ever have a chance to be. We are perfectionists in nearly everything we do. When it comes to getting better, though, neither of us is exceptionally good at improving without an outside perspective. A big part in the process of lesson improvement is having a trusted support group who pushes and encourages you to get better. If you don't have this type of support group at your school, we suggest reaching out to

---

8   $P \Rightarrow \neg \neg P$ Double negation: If a statement is true, then it's not the case that the statement is not true.

this incredible group of math teachers: bit.ly/mtbosdirectory.

Lest you think we're perfect teachers—or charlatans—we *do* practice what we preach.

Ask for Input from Other Teachers

"Mandy, I need to talk to you. I sucked again."

Those words, in one rendition or another, might as well have been on repeat during my (John's) first two years of teaching. Mandy was our literacy coach for the school, but she was so much more for me—she was my mentor. Fortunately, Mandy kept me afloat by helping me keep my job, my sanity, and my love of showing up to work. When I needed to vent, she listened. When I had questions, she answered. When I wanted to improve a lesson, she let me bounce ideas off her, and they always came back to me even better.

Mandy's outside perspective helped me turn "good" lessons into masterfully and thoughtfully prepared entrées the kids would receive well. Those early years of teaching were sprinkled—no, *saturated*—with lessons where I'd overestimated my classes' ability (or desire) to grasp the objective in the manner or within the timeframe I'd allotted. In spite of how much I disliked my undergrad credential program, hindsight tells me a class on "how to effectively prepare a lesson without screwing up your students" would have helped a whole lot. Fortunately, Mandy was there to add some kick to my early lessons.

About to teach a lesson on decimal operations, I wanted to do something different, something unique. I told her I planned to draw a bunch of products on the board, give the kids a budget, and they would purchase enough items to get up to, but not over, the budget. *Awesome!*

And then Mandy gave me her perspective.[9] She suggested I cut out little pictures of each product and put them on the board. Students

---

9   Bouncing ideas off someone is a huge benefit; it will make your lessons better. To go along with that, there will be times when you realize that your idea was awful. Be okay with that.

would go to the board to "shop" for their items, glue them onto a paper, and write a story about all the fun they had going camping with those items.

The lesson was a hit. Thanks to Mandy's guidance and support, I prepared my educational kitchen with guidelines for coming to the

---

If I ask for input only from teachers in my content area, my lessons will never be truly diverse and inclusive.

---

board, asking for items, and knowing when it was appropriate to go shopping, as well as what the story could (and could not) involve. Because of her, my "table" was well-defined and respected by the students. Without her input, I would've been destined for another *Mandy-I-need-to-talk-to-you-I-sucked-again* day.

The best thing I learned from working with Mandy is that if I ask for input only from teachers in my content area, my lessons will never be truly diverse and inclusive.

Seek Out Mentors and Coaches

What's the deal? I (Matt) wondered one day, between periods.

Why aren't they as stoked about this as I am?

By now, you've likely noticed it's quite common for us to be more excited than the students in our class. But this lesson ranks as one of my top five,[10] so I was confused by the lack of interest. Unfortunately,

---

10 In case you're curious:
1. Mullet Ratio
2. Barbie Bungee
3. Megalodon
4. Inequalities on the Number Line or Home Depot (It's a tie.)
5. Trig Ratios Using Sextants

although my students *should've* been excited, they were treating this day like just any other Thursday in April.[11]

Toward the end of a unit on graphing (using a prescribed curriculum which left some holes), we took a couple days to do Barbie Bungee.[12] Similar to John's description of Barbie Zipline, we showed a bungee video, discussed the important elements of a bungee jump, and decided that the ideal jump has Barbie coming *really* close to the ground, but not touching it.

Safe, yet fun.

We prepped our rubber band bungee cords and went outside to measure some trial bungee jumps. After finding the most fun—but still safe—jump for a small height, medium height, and tall height, students recorded their data on the worksheet, which was freshly redesigned.

It pained me to delete my beautiful table from previous years, and though I knew the lesson was improved, something about the new procedure felt…lacking. Compared to the two prior years, this activity was completely overhauled. When I say *completely*, I mean *my brain was a bit fried from making sense of the prescribed curriculum, and I forgot what students care about and forgot what is mathematically important.* Not until my math coach came to visit did I realize what was missing: The Point.

Barbie Bungee was a fun activity, but it had no point, no *boom!*

The previous year, we bungeed after the state test, but now, I had stuck it in the middle of a unit without crafting student tasks around a learning goal. The pink lab sheet and fun activity were just more disjointed operations with no attachment to the larger world of mathematics.

---

11 Established teachers are probably snorting and saying, "It's April. *That's* why they were uninspired." While it's definitely harder to get the juice moving in the spring, it's no excuse for us teachers to phone it in—especially not beginning to coast at spring break and drifting in neutral until June.

12 MrVaudrey.com/barbiebungee14

This is the very thing I seek to avoid.[13]

My math coach burst into my class at lunch. "The big jump! That's the point. The students gather data to derive an equation to solve for the height which Barbie needs to jump from so she doesn't die. That's your point."

But there was an issue. My students gathered their own data. Glancing over their shoulders while they worked made my stomach tense. Their data collection was pitiful, so the numbers didn't work well together, which meant their equations were all over the place. One group calculated they would need eight rubber bands to jump off the roof (after they figured jumping off a desk required six bands), and another group needed 100 bands to jump off the roof.

Well, crap! I scrapped bungee for the day.

On Monday morning, I weighed all the dolls on a food scale. Taking one from each weight category outside, I conducted my own Barbie bungee jumps, recorded my own data points (more than three apiece) and dropped them into Desmos, which has quickly become my go-to device for concretizing something that's too abstract.[14] The table had

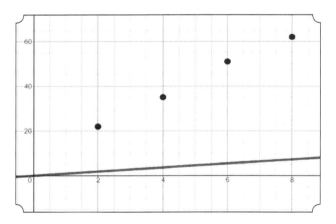

---

13 You know that scene in *Star Wars III: Revenge of the Sith*, when Anakin chokes Padmé and begins to realize that he's become the very evil he fought against? It was kinda like that.

14 To see the interactive calculator, check out mrvaudrey.com/barbiedesmos.

been set when I had data points for each weight category, ready to be matched to a line.

When the students arrived to first period, I called on them to change the slope and y-intercept of the line, one doll at a time.

"Jonathan, should the slope increase, decrease, or stay the same?"

"Maria, should the y-intercept increase, decrease, or stay the same?"

"Alex, should the slope increase, decrease, or stay the same?"

Students during every period were silent as they saw firsthand in real time what "increase the slope of a line" meant. Also, there was no "right answer." You wanna move the y-intercept down? Fine. The next student might move it right back up.

Can you imagine doing this by hand?[15]

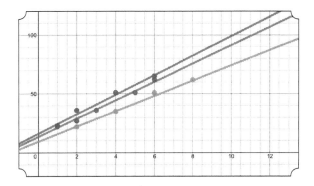

Eventually, students agreed that each line passed through the respective points (for the most part), and we dropped the values into an equation for the number of bungees needed (r) to jump a certain height (h). I passed out my Barbies to each group, and each Barbie matched an equation from a Barbie in a similar weight class.

---

15 Completed graph at mrvaudrey.com/barbiecomplete. You know what I like most about that graph? You can make little tweaks here and there and still be correct. What a great way to talk about error and accuracy with your students. Math is messy and awesome.

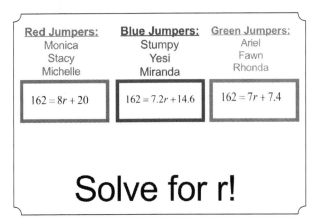

We spent most of the class time discussing how to fit the line to the data and why.

I'm okay with that.

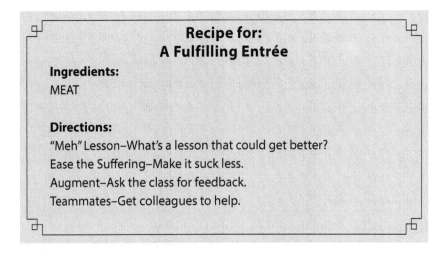

Side Dishes

We *love* side dishes. As good as a New York strip steak, a plate of chicken parmesan, or an eggplant burger piled high with veggies may taste, isolated on a plate, those entrées lack interest. One of the best steaks John ever ate was served on an incredibly hot plate, cooked to a perfect medium rare, and seasoned in a way which drove him to go to the kitchen and kiss the chef.[1] But the side dishes are what *really* made the meal exceptional. The baked potato was sized, buttered, and dressed to perfectly complement the steak. The asparagus couldn't have been any better—crispy, with a little bit of olive oil, sea salt, and crushed pepper. And the side salad neutralized the palate, rounding off the entrée, creating a meal he will never forget.

And for the carb junkies out there—like Matt—you know that a special kind of joy arrives when the server brings the bread basket. Though Matt can polish off an entire loaf on his own (and still finish his wife's leftovers), he knows he probably shouldn't.

Side dishes—including deliciously buttered, fresh-baked bread—are mouthwatering additions to any entrée, but are meant to be consumed sparingly (whether with a restaurant meal or with your math class equivalent). Too many math "carbs," and your class feels bloated and needs to take a nap. Get the combination right, though, and you'll *wow* your students with an unforgettable lesson.

---

1 And now I'm not allowed in Sizzler anymore. Paolo, I'm sorry. I was overcome with positive feelings.

CHAPTER 13
THE WORLD NEEDS MORE EDUCATION GEEKS

Side dishes are the most fun part of teaching—the barometer that identifies the teachers who will do anything to help students learn. Costumes, loud music, standing on desks, baking cookies with a solar oven on the blacktop—these are the side dishes the "crazy teacher" uses to make entrées more meaningful.

Matt is that crazy teacher.

"Why is Mr. Vaudrey wearing a kilt?"

"Oh, he's teaching coordinate transformations today."

Fawn Nguyen, a teacher in Southern California, loves teaching, kids, and math. Unashamedly. Her classroom runs like a Swiss watch. Her students develop teamwork and problem-solving skills *far* beyond those of average sixth graders because, in her class, risk takes center stage. For example, she routinely gives students geometry tools and no directions, and then asks for advanced constructions.

Sometimes, when you're a math teacher, especially a middle school math teacher, your students' mindset about math can affect you. Matt admits that he did not love math. In fact, he bragged about being a geek with I'm a math teacher as his excuse for that geekiness.[2] But really, being a geek isn't all that bad. Take a look at what actor Simon Pegg says:

Being a geek is all about being honest about what you enjoy and not being afraid to demonstrate that affection. It means never having to play it cool about how much you like something. It's basically a license to proudly emote on a some-what childish level rather than behave like a supposed adult. Being a geek is extremely liberating.[3]

The world needs more crazy teachers—more adults who are passionate about getting kids excited about school and learning. The world needs more education geeks.

Ever been at a party and chatted with a stranger? The stranger starts with, "So, what do you do?" As soon as we say "teacher," the stranger begins to unload about an awful teacher he had and how—twenty years later—he *still* hates the subject taught by the teacher.

We're sick of that.

You're sick of that, too. That's why you're knee-deep in a book about making your class more meaningful. And while you can't change the

THE WORLD NEEDS MORE CRAZY TEACHERS—MORE ADULTS WHO ARE PASSIONATE ABOUT GETTING KIDS EXCITED ABOUT SCHOOL AND LEARNING.

culture of education all by yourself, you can change *your* classroom for a hundred or so kids a year. Make your classroom exciting. Use costumes, music, go outside, and present weird lessons. Make class *meaningful.*

---

2 In recent years, the term *geek* has been adopted as a badge by enthusiasts: car geek, beer geek, fashion geek, dance geek. It turns out that being a *geek* was cool all along.

3 Picture him reading that in his Scottish accent.

Because some adults don't understand how important it is for school to be interesting. In fact, some adults—and this is criminal—use academics to *punish* kids. Is it any wonder some of those students hate going to school?

The Joy of Learning or "How to Make Kids Hate School"

"Stop!"

A whimper from across the terminal in the Ontario, California, airport made us look up from our conversation about Google Forms. The young boy, no more than twelve years old, made eye contact with us before he buried his face in his book and pleaded to the woman on his right, "Stop! Please!"

We'd seen this before: an upset mother reprimanding her son. The son upset his mom, and now he'll feel her wrath. Many parents have been there—kids driving them crazy, and they make an empty threat that they have no intention of following through.

"You're gonna be grounded for a year! And no video games! And you're doing dishes for six weeks! And you'll sleep on a bed made of pinecones! And I'm putting peanut butter in your PlayStation!"

Sadly, this was far from silly.

The woman folded her arms and replied flatly, "You just made it four hundred. Wanna try for four-fifty?"

The boy put his book down and turned to look at the woman, probably his mother. "Stop!" he pleaded again.

"Four-fifty, it is. Let's go for six," she bristled, sitting up straighter in her chair as her son scooted lower and lower. "Six hundred it is. You wanna stop crying now?"

The boy glanced at us again, his face growing red and his prepubescent hands squeezing the pages of a Captain Underpants book. The book flopped onto his lap and he whispered, "Stop...please."

"Seven hundred sentences." Mom stared down her son, a hint of pride in her voice, which was loud enough for us to hear from our seats in the row facing them. When we heard the word "sentences," both of us gripped our chairs' pleather-wrapped armrests. *This woman was assigning sentences to her son as punishment.*

This wasn't the first time we'd seen a novice wrestle with the will of an adolescent. Unfortunately, we see it in classrooms, as well. It wasn't even the first time we'd seen someone use *writing* as corporal punishment and feel confident it was the right move. Matt even did that his entire first year teaching.[4] But this was the first time in recent memory we were powerless to do anything about it.

"You need to stop being oppositional. You're twelve years old, and I expect you to listen. There! you just made it eight hundred!" Mom was determined to win.

The book covered the boy's face again. "I'm not gonna write them," he sobbed into the pages.

"What's that?" His mom held a hand up to her ear, a hint of sarcasm tinted her voice. "Do I hear nine hundred?"

This scenario was a microcosm of hundreds—maybe thousands—of conversations that happen on a regular basis. Likely, every night, young men and women are being served math problems, sentences, and spelling punishments by their parents for some reason or another. Regardless of race, social class, or religion, parents are handing out a *disdain for learning* because it's the most readily available (non-physical) punishment they have.[5]

"I'm not gonna write them!" he was insisting by then, tears starting to roll down his face, trying to convince his mom—or convince himself. We couldn't tell.

This mother of a pubescent preteen had made the decision giving her son sentences to write was a viable punishment for whatever he had done wrong prior to boarding their flight to Oakland on a Tuesday night in May. Before this mom had started ramping up scholastic

---

4   Ack. I know; not proud of it.

5   Teachers use it, too. See mrvaudrey.com/uglyexboyfriend.

consequences, it had been yet another empty airport with the faint sounds of CNN mixed with the light smell of Cinnabon. This conversation was now turning our stomachs.

"One. Thousand. Sentences." Her head bobbed with each word and she leaned in close to him. He whimpered and leaned away.

John growled in Matt's ear, "I can't sit here for this." We angrily zipped our bags and stormed to the other end of Gate 29. We didn't storm off because we were avoiding her; we walked away because we both wanted to intervene, but knew we'd only make the boy's situation worse.

John leaned in and said, "You know, a *younger* John would've said something to her. Like 'Hey, you're training your son to hate school if you use sentences as punishment, so knock it off!' A *younger* John would've let her have it."

A shrill voice interrupted him. "You're up to a thousand now. I told you that I'll keep going, right?"

John looked at the ceiling and gritted his teeth. "Did she raise her voice? It feels like she's raising her voice so we can all hear her."

"Eleven hundred. Twelve hundred." She was no longer pausing between numbers. Determined to win, the pile of punishment paper grew larger and larger in her mind.

"Mom! I'm not gonna write that many sentences! This isn't *fair!*" The boy was sobbing heavily at this point, red in the face and uncertain of what he could possibly do to dig himself out of this pit.

Matt rubbed his temples. "Younger John is looking pretty good right now. Getting older isn't fun if you're supposed to tolerate bad treatment of teenagers. But you know telling her off won't help her improve."

"You know what I shoulda done?" John was so angry, he hardly heard Matt. "I shoulda said, 'Lady, we can go talk in private, or I can tell you what I'm thinking *in front of* your son. I've seen many young men and women turned away from learning because of *that* punishment. Rather than having your son write sentences, how about *having a conversation* with him about his decisions, how he coulda made adjustments, and letting *him* choose the punishment, *huh*?' That's what I *shoulda* said! I still might!"

John's eyes were alight and his jaw was clenched. Not a violent or angry man by nature, his blood boils when he sees power abused and, as a stocky athlete with a beard, he's a sight to behold when he's angry.

We lined up to board our flight and asked the attendant how full the plane was. He shrugged, "Only, like, 38 out of 140," and waved us on.

Perfect. A ratio problem to distract us.

We tried to chat about something else—*anything* else. Matt tried a dopey grin. "Well, thirty-five is five sevens and one forty is twenty sevens, so…"

John sighed. "Five out of twenty—the plane is about twenty-five or thirty percent full, yeah?"

We rounded the jetway corner and saw the woman seated in a row by herself. A dozen rows further back, a small head of curly black hair looked out the window and sniffled. He was asserting some independence sitting by himself, or, at the very least, avoiding further punishment.

We settled into our seats across the aisle from the woman—just in case the opportunity arose to talk about parenting with a woman ten years our senior. We both have wives who would've pulled our sleeves and said, "Let it go. She's not going to change based on a conversation with some guy on a plane."

For the next seventy-five minutes, we both silently dwelled on the question: What could we *possibly* say in that instance to change her mind?

Ding

"Welcome to Ontario Airport. Local time is 10:35 p.m."

We unbuckled our seatbelts and pulled down our bags.

There are times when the less painful option is just to bite your tongue.

This scenario is not unique to airports, and certainly not unique to the learners who carry baggage[6] through our doors on a daily basis. Unfortunately, it's likely that the use of academics as punishment happens more frequently in homes where our underserved and disadvantaged students live.

With that said, one of our biggest challenges is to welcome the young man above (and other young men and women in similar situations) into our classroom merely hours after being dealt a verbal lashing in front of total strangers.

Or maybe she just watched somebody get beat up during her walk to school.

Or maybe he had to walk his cousin to school since his mom got deported.

Or maybe she fled the house at midnight last night when her dad came home drunk.

On any given day, our neediest students are trying to make sense of difficult situations on top of any new learning they're about to encounter during the regularly scheduled school day.

Now consider this scenario: That student arrives in your class. She knows what to expect because you've *Set the Table* (Chapter 3), she's engaged quickly with an *Appetizer* (Chapter 4)—and you've got a table full of barbies and rope for some reason. Let's be clear: The mood of this student will likely be sour anyway, but at least she has one place in her world that is safe and where she is valued. She can still love learning, thanks to the environment you've created.

Seeing their teacher take a big risk on a lesson could very well serve the souls of kids in those situations. It could be the *one thing* they needed to tie their shoes, strap on their backpacks, and make their way to school for the day. Or it could be the one part of their day that sucks a little less. For the preteen in the airport or the surly student in the front row, we can make our classrooms a safe space for all of our learners.

---

6 Pun very intended.

Perhaps some normalcy is precisely what's needed to keep them going.

Chapter 14
Make Your Lessons Pop

We've shared stories and examples of ways we've worked to kick it up a notch or two—or ten—in our classrooms. The elements to make our lessons pop are side dishes. Much like the steak dinner, a perfectly cooked steak by itself, eaten by yourself, on a cold plate, is still lonely. Side dishes complete the meal and make it pop.

In our classrooms, side dishes aren't just about what's on the plate. The *pop* also comes from who is at the table, what we were celebrating—the entire atmosphere. Sure, we can set the table in a way that gets kids interested—be it a mullet ratio, a zipline, a billboard, a regular day solving systems of linear equations—or any other ideas we've shared. But to really make the lesson pop, we gotta have the side dishes.

Here are side dishes that complete a lesson and make it pop:

- Earning shock value with a mullet haircut is a side dish.

- Playing songs with the word "circle" in the title is a side dish.[1]

- Sending action figures and dolls cruising down a zipline made of fishing line is a side dish.

- Going outside to pace out the length of a megalodon is a side dish.

- Having a cross-town mathematical showdown on Google Hangouts is a side dish.[2]

- Showing a short YouTube video of guys bungee jumping into an abandoned Russian missile silo is a side dish.[3]

Side dishes take the most time to prepare. Seasoning a steak and cooking it takes, at most, sixteen minutes in the right conditions. However, prepping and baking a potato, roasting asparagus, and chopping veggies for the salad take much more time and patience to do it right. While preparing your lesson, ask yourself a few questions:

What can I do to make this lesson more powerful?

How am I going to engage my students?

Where do I start?

WHAT CAN I DO TO MAKE THIS LESSON MORE POWERFUL?

Steak is good.[4] Steak and potatoes are good. But steak, garlic mashed potatoes, roasted Brussels sprouts, carrots, and a side salad? That's *beyond* good.

---

1   On the day, that we learned circumference and area of a circle.

2   classroomchef.com/hangingout

3   MrVaudrey.com/barbiebungee

4   Unless you're a vegan. Is there something like Tofurky, but tofu-steak? Tofake? Ha! It's got "fake" in the name! That's perfect. Somebody call Jennie-O. (We're both carnivores, but know vegans we love and appreciate.)

Teaching ratios? Barely good, even if you nail it. Teaching ratios with a mullet ratio is good, as long as you fully commit; otherwise, it's just a silly lesson. But a Mullet Ratio lesson, complete with a haircut, costume, silly photos, loud music, and students measuring each other's hair with pipe cleaners? That's bound to catch all students.

How Am I Going to Engage My Students?

As of this writing, *engagement* is thrown around a lot as an educational buzzword. It certainly isn't a bad word to use regarding education, but we tend to agree with our friend Karl Lindgren-Streicher who says, "Curiosity is far more powerful than engagement."[5]

We can *engage* our students by wearing a funny costume for fifty-five minutes, but making them *curious* about why ratios work the way they do is more complicated. Plus, it's more likely to leave a lasting impression.

The focus of side dishes isn't on *engagement*, but on *commitment*. Being committed is going beyond the variety of synthetic, prepackaged lessons dependent on cute graphics, math raps, or building *papier-mâché* everything. While none of those things are harmful to class culture if they are the supplements, they shouldn't be the centerpiece. The side dish is meant to complement the entrée, not to replace it. If your kids fill up on crafts and cute graphics but miss the point of the lesson, they aren't retaining anything.

Be *committed* to reaching all students by any means necessary. Teaching is a noble profession, and to keep it that way, help students learn your class content so the benefits last long after they leave your classroom.[6] Be intentional about piquing their curiosity so that they *want* to really dive into the content and explore it for themselves.

---

5   Find him on Twitter @LS_Karl.
6   "Teaching" is often confused with "helping students learn content." Each can exist separately.

Where Do I Start?

Getting your students excited about your class—so curious that they can't wait to show up every day—takes work. And if you're in damage-control mode right now, that reality can feel overwhelming.

Our advice: Start small.

Doing a complete overhaul on the pacing guide is sure to add stress to you and put your students into panic mode (because even if your class has been boring, your kids have a small sense of comfort in knowing what to expect). By starting small, you can implement Wacky Wednesdays, or something equally corny. Planted firmly in the middle of the week, a side dish will build momentum and make the week easier to finish. Check out these ideas to get your brain moving in the right direction:

- Rearrange the desks for that one day.
- Wear a costume or clothing to introduce the day's theme.[7]
- Give a hat/necklace/shield/wand to a student to wear or use as the maestro of the morning's appetizer.
- Ask two students to come to the board each morning to respond to the day's prompt.
- Show a video clip that (even loosely) relates to the day's lesson.
- Toss a beach ball to the kids you want to answer questions. (Maybe even wear swim trunks and put some zinc oxide on your nose.)
- Participate in a video chat with another class about the day's warm-up (pre-planning required here, but it's pretty awesome).
- Read the lyrics to a pop song like it's a beat poem, right when the bell rings.[8]

---

7   A teacher in Matt's MEd program had a whole arsenal of ties and chose them based on what unit the class was studying.

8   In a charter school with no bells, half the class was tardy all the time. After Matt started doing this, students began jogging to class to catch the "Dramatic Reading" of the day.

- Introduce a lesson without speaking. Pre-write slides (for the projector) or cue cards with your message and silently point to them.[9]

- Get a ridiculous mullet haircut.

- Tell the class you're heading outside.

- Find a video—or an image—more engaging than you are.

- Set up a grocery store to drive home decimals.

- Go ziplining.

- Build something as a class.

- Play a song that means "send someone to the back of class to get calculators."[10]

- Go on a field trip—even a local one.

- Invite a guest speaker to class.

- Dress in bubble-wrap and a helmet and act skittish all day, insisting, "Guys. Inertia can kill you!"[11]

- Dress up as a pig the day students draw pictorial representations.[12]

- Stand on a desk during the lesson, instead of on the floor. Why not?[13]

---

9 And watch as your students also get silent. Or as they read the sentences aloud, if they're elementary ages.

10 MrVaudrey.com/music

11 Middle school science teacher (and good friend and Pinterest goddess) Ashley Northington from Guam dressed in a bike helmet and bubble wrap. "Guys!" She deadpanned. "Inertia…can *kill* you! I'm taking no chances." Then she timidly crawled out from under her desk and started class.

12 Mrs. McAvoy, kindergarten teacher. Get it? *Pig-torial?* I hope your students already know how to spell *pictorial*, though.

13 Based on experience, *highly* recommend doing this *after* confirming the stability of the desk.

- Video-chat with someone in the field you're studying and play "Twenty Questions" to have students guess the person's job.[14]

- On review day, have a Review Scavenger Hunt spanning the entire campus.

- Dress as a doctor and model "Prep-position" (on the desk, under the desk, inside the desk, etc.).[15]

- Hold a tasting party and serve food from the region you're studying.

- Get students to touch something gross, then talk about why it's important.[16]

- Light a candle and then take a bite.[17]

These ideas and many more challenge you—the leader of your room—to take a risk. *Engaging* your students does not require you to do a stand-up comedy routine or dress in an absurd outfit or cut your hair.[18] Find something that works for you and the lesson. None of them demand you to abandon the lesson; instead, they demand attention for it. If venturing from the work that you've put together is intimidating, these ideas (and more below) can help lessen those fears and encourage welcoming risk into your lesson preparation.[19]

---

14 Called a "Mystery Skype." See Jo-Ann Fox (@AppEducationFox) or Scott Bedley (@ScotTeach) for examples.

15 mrvaudrey.com/prep-position

16 They'll squeal and turn up their nose, but *every* student will wanna touch the squid. Seriously—even Brittany.

17 The candle is cut from a potato and the wick is an almond. Get students discussing the difference between *observation* and *inference*.

18 But if you do all three of those at once, email us a picture.

19 For even *more* side dishes and lesson starters, check out Dave Burgess' book, *Teach Like a PIRATE*.

EMBRACE THE UNEXPECTED

While looking for a lesson about the Triangle Sum Theorem,[20] I (John) searched the word "triangle" on YouTube. Somehow, I stumbled onto a video about place value and a customer calling Verizon Wireless to complain about a discrepancy in his bill.[21] As I watched the video, the palms of my hands started sweating. I started to lean into the computer screen. There was tension, turmoil, and turbulence, all in an audio recording lasting less than three minutes. Following the first viewing, and after calming down a little, I replayed the video to make sure this was the best thing for my students. Yep, it was!

My students had been struggling with place value—even as sophomores in high school—so this was a perfect fit. Some might say, "Certainly your geometry students don't need to waste their time talking about place value." On the contrary, everyone—including us—could use an occasional refresher on place value.

The video was on the screen, paused, when the students arrived in class. Once again, the "wait, what are we doing today?" started to fill the room. The bell rang, which meant it was time to watch how other people reacted to an audio recording destined to be a classic. As the customer went through his defense and the customer service representative struggled with the concept of unit conversion, the students became restless. About forty-one seconds into the video, as the caller grew frustrated, Jordan mumbled, "This dude needs help." But the stress only got heavier. Moans and groans about how hard this guy was trying to convey his math and the error of the service reps grew louder by the second—until the manager said, "I don't know, I'm not a mathematician," at the 2:22 mark.

---

20 The concept that all interior angle measures of a triangle must add up to 180 degrees.

21 To be honest, I have no idea how this video came across the screen. If you haven't seen it, please take the time to enjoy (and possibly get frustrated, develop empathy for either side, or cry): classroomchef.com/pennies.

Shelby couldn't take it anymore and declared to anyone who would listen: "Geez, someone should help these people."

Why yes, Shelby. Yes, they should.

So we did.

The prompt was simple: Assuming you had the ability to video-conference with the Verizon customer service team, how would you explain the customer's frustration and mathematical justification?

After students quickly and passionately developed a diagram (or two), they were certain would help, they discussed unit conversion,

---

THE OPPOSITE OF *BORED* ISN'T *ENTERTAINED*; IT'S *CURIOUS.*

---

talked about place value, and critiqued the reasoning of others—all without needing a prompt from me. YouTube provided the motivation; all I had to do was press *play*.

DO I HAVE TO TEACH THIS WAY EVERY DAY?

Someone decided how to present the lessons in your classroom. It could be that your team determined a particular lesson was the easiest way to deliver the material. Or maybe you saw a lesson online somewhere and thought it would be fun to duplicate in your classroom. Or perhaps a particular approach was mandated by your administrator. We understand that you probably work with a team of teachers, and you don't want to burn any bridges by demanding an immediate, complete overhaul of how every lesson is taught in your department. We get it.

That's why we recommend when you're working on building allegiance and buy-in with your department (and your class) that you start small. Try one of the suggestions listed in the "Where Do I Start?"

section above, or search Pinterest or Google for an idea to help you reach your next learning goal. Add side dishes to your classroom slowly and watch your students and department get excited and hungry for more.

The truth is, every day doesn't need to be a five-star experience. Plenty of three- and four-star days populate our plan books, and that's okay. In fact, there are some "leftovers" and "take-out" days, too. You want a lesson that's easy to deliver? Awesome. As we mentioned at the beginning of the book, *teaching is hard*. Bringing your best for 180 days is incredibly difficult. Some days need to be easier than others. To that end, side dishes serve two purposes:

1.) SIDE DISHES MAKE CLASS FUN FOR STUDENTS.

The correlation between learning and boredom isn't founded on logic; it's founded on our own experiences as students—some experience being decades old. The reality is that even if you, as the teacher, think something is boring, you don't have to present it that way.

The purpose of a side dish is to make class a little more fun and get students a little more interested in attending. Even if—at first—only a few of your students get curious, their enthusiasm will be contagious. Plus, administrators love to hear students ask one another, "What do you think we'll do in class today?"

2.) SIDE DISHES MAKE CLASS FUN FOR TEACHERS.

During Matt's first year of teaching, his mom told him, "If you're bored, the kids are *definitely* bored." It's so true.

If you're midway through a lesson and think, "*Bleh. I'm bored*," say so. Out loud! Your students will be shocked:

"What did he say?"

"Can he say that?"

"Is he allowed to be bored?"

When you recognize that you are bored, immediately stop doing or saying whatever's boring and serve up a side dish that makes the lesson a little more interesting—for both you and your students.[22] They'll engage and may even leave with some of that lesson tucked away in their brains. Remember: The opposite of bored isn't entertained; it's curious.

Believe us, your students are curious about whether there is a more interesting way to deal with the concept of percentage mixture problems.[23] They'll be curious to know how many monomial cubes fit in a sack or what percentage of their life is taken up each class period. Being *curious* leads directly to interest and fun. Teachers expose students to the world and let them wonder.[24]

Class should be a time for fun and exploration and interest.

Lots of people have boring jobs—jobs that require words like *cubicle* and *expense report* and *management training*. Teachers—conversely—get to help students explore and discover in a well-lit room, crafting experiences with *nearly complete autonomy*, guided only by a loose grouping of learning goals, and supported by a staff which does the most administrative parts of our job.[25]

It's a wonder the entire country doesn't want to be teachers.

It's the best job ever.

---

22 "Okay, people. Stand up, talk to your neighbor, tell them everything you know about logarithms, and then we'll compare notes. Go."

23 Mary Bourrassa's blog post and lessons about percentage mixture problems are, by far, the best we've seen.

24 For more on this, read Max Ray and Annie Fetter (both on MathForum.org) and Michael Fentor (ReasonAndWonder.com).

25 The homies at the district office who sit in cubicles and file expense reports before heading off to management training. Mad respect, y'all. Somebody's gotta do it.

Recipe for:
Side Dishes Add SPICE

Ingredients:

Spontaneous–Students never know what to expect.

Public–Make a scene, be silly, get outside.

Interest–Beyond *engaged*, get students **curious**.

Class is fun for students *and* teachers.

Excited–Be a geek, be unashamedly awesome.

Directions:

Start small. A prop, a costume, a video. Sprinkle in flavor to taste. Season liberally as students get more curious and more excited.

DESSERTS

At a meal, in the classroom, or at the end of a Tarantino movie, we all want the same thing: closure. We want everything to wrap up nicely—and for that smug jerk with the cowboy boots to go to jail. In the Tarantino movie, not in the classroom.

When we think of closure for a meal, we think of *dessert*—where something sweet kicks on the pleasure receptors in the brain, and we drive home with the pleasant hum in our ears only *Fudge Oreo Cheesecake* can produce. In the classroom, we call it *assessment*—and it's usually tough to swallow.

Let's change that.

CHAPTER 15
RETHINKING ASSESSMENT

A t its core, assessment (which, because that term puts us to sleep, we'll call "gathering" in this chapter) addresses two challenges: providing closure to a lesson and gathering information about the success of the lesson. Gathering is definitely more likely to lock in meaning to the day's activity than our shouting at students as they leave, "Do problems twelve through twenty tonight for homework! It's due tomorrowwwwwww!"

To combat the drudgery of gathering, many teachers have subscribed to the belief that a project is better than an assessment. After all, if a student can use the information learned in class in conjunction with their creative skill set, surely the learning is destined to increase. With that, students get their project outline from the teacher and head home to beg their parents for a ride to the office supply store so they can buy materials necessary for an "A+" by following the usual guidelines:

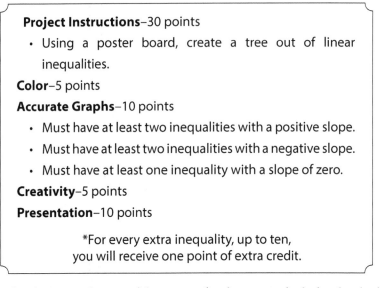

Project Instructions–30 points
- Using a poster board, create a tree out of linear inequalities.

Color–5 points

Accurate Graphs–10 points
- Must have at least two inequalities with a positive slope.
- Must have at least two inequalities with a negative slope.
- Must have at least one inequality with a slope of zero.

Creativity–5 points

Presentation–10 points

*For every extra inequality, up to ten,
you will receive one point of extra credit.

The cherry on the top of this recipe for disaster is the kids who don't enjoy art will find someone who does and ask for "help" with their project. Then students who *clearly* didn't do the writing on their poster board give the excuse, "Her handwriting is way better than mine. But I did all the work."[1] And if that wasn't enough, twenty percent of the class translates "creativity" into "make some cool swirly glue trails and douse them with glitter."[2]

The boundaries we provide—disguised not-so-cleverly as instructions—tell students exactly what we value. In the example above, we are giving 33.3 percent of the grade to students based on their ability to be "creative." No wonder many of them assume a poster board adorned with glitter and three dozen colors is the only way to showcase creativity. Another 33.3 percent is based on a presentation—easy for the teacher to grade. Each student stands in front of the classroom, reads his poster, and sits down. And the process is repeated thirty-five more times, five or six periods in a row.

---

1 Often the same student who asked to work in groups in the first place. What a wonder.

2 We hate glitter. Impossible to clean up, sharp in your eye, and expensive. Why do people still use this miserable product?

And two-thirds of the project points have nothing to do with math at all.

Putting all of this into context makes us wonder: How much good are we really doing by requiring students to bring, and many times grading them on, a *narrow scope of creativity defined by the instructor* into their school projects? Is the data from a poster project any better than a quiz or test? There will always be posters, ten-question quizzes, and digital versions of slideshows. But we can do better. Let's define *gathering* as more than poster projects. Before we do that, though, we need to understand where our students are coming from.

THEORY OF RELATIVITY

Some time ago, I (John) stumbled onto a video from Malcolm Gladwell about relativity.[3] It wasn't Einstein, but it was genius. In the video, Gladwell discusses the fact that our perception of ourselves is based on the attributes of the people who surround us. In a crowd of musicians, I am the worst at playing an instrument. In a daycare, I am the best baseball player in the room. This got me thinking. We compare ourselves to the people in our cohort, no matter who the cohort is. We want to see how we measure up.

"Stairway to Heaven" is a musical masterpiece—full of memorization and rhythm, beauty, and passion—that very few can replicate. Can you play it?

Gearheads can name every part of a motor and its role in making the combustion engine move a vehicle forward. Can you?

Makeup artists routinely match the best shade of lipstick for their customers, oftentimes knowing each shade's name and its relation to other shades. Do you?

Actors can memorize and recite—with true replication and passion—a Shakespearean monologue, time and time again. Can you?

---

3 I strongly encourage setting aside the 19:14 minutes it takes to watch Malcolm Gladwell's Zeitgeist Americas 2013 video.

Historians have built maps so elaborate that they are laced with historical relevance and precision. Some have the ability to memorize entire maps, even multiple maps, as a way of navigating and creating better worlds. Are you able to do the same?

An NFL playbook includes seven hundred to eight hundred pages of plays—just for the offense. These individuals run those plays and execute their routes or assignments with precision while being under ridiculous amounts of stress. Could you?

Human beings have over six hundred muscles in their body. Some people can identify each one from memory and describe its function. Can you? Even half? A quarter?

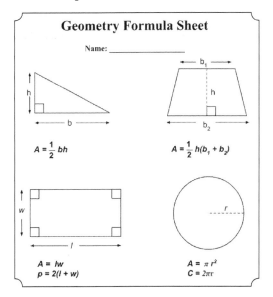

Geometry Formula Sheet

Name: _____

$A = \frac{1}{2}bh$

$A = \frac{1}{2}h(b_1 + b_2)$

$A = lw$
$p = 2(l + w)$

$A = \pi r^2$
$C = 2\pi r$

Now, stare at this sheet. Memorize it. Come back tomorrow and let's have a quiz on this. Personally, I would *dominate* that quiz. In fact, I'll get every question correct.

We have students in our classes every single day who excel as musicians, gearheads, artists, designers, athletes, etc. Their intelligence is evident, as is their individuality, but if they can't memorize and repeat information from a chart or textbook, their assessments read: *below basic, failing,* or *at-risk.* And that assessment leads them to believe they are dumb because they can't regurgitate twenty math standards on a standardized test.

Instead of reprimanding students based on their grades in school, we can value their abilities in something they are passionate about. There is no easy fix to the education system, to grades, or to making kids feel welcome. But if we can somehow show them what they are

---

IF WE CAN SOMEHOW SHOW THEM WHAT THEY ARE DOING IS AMAZING, WE MIGHT BE ABLE TO PRODUCE BETTER PEOPLE.

---

doing is amazing, we might be able to produce better people. Forget the fluffy, feel-good anecdotes. This is an opportunity to show students that four core subjects don't dictate their overall intelligence.

One student told me near the beginning of the year he was a failure because he failed a test and, as a result, wound up with a temporary "F" in my class. When I asked him what he liked to do, his immediate response was playing the guitar. He was shocked I didn't know the first thing about how to play. He was smarter than me—by a lot.

I want my kids to know they are smarter than me about something.

LEARNING FROM OUR STUDENTS

"Good morning, class. Remember, we're taking a quiz today. Go ahead and clear your desks of everything except a pencil and your brilliance."

We'd spent the past two weeks learning about parallel lines and transversals in geometry, and I was pretty sure my students had it nailed down.[4] Walking around the room allowed me to see how my students were doing, what questions they might have had, and how amazing the brain in motion really was. It was fascinating to watch a kid work through a problem with multiple steps to come to a solution.

---

4 Hey, we've *all* had our naïve teacher moments.

As I looked across the room, I saw Russell. Russell was the sophomore who'd slogged through nine years, two months, and three weeks of public education—getting knocked down every step of the way. However, his peers weren't doing the bullying. Russell—unfortunately—was being "bullied" by the educational system.

Russell had an IEP[5] he couldn't understand (because very few followed it), but somewhere along the line, someone thought he had a disability. And you couldn't ask him what his accommodations were—they were rarely addressed and even more rarely monitored. Russell was a product of poor public education bureaucracy, and we were the ones to blame. Yet he was the one who carried the branding of a "far below basic" learner.

Working on his third problem of the day, he looked back at me. He was a big kid with naturally puffy and set-back eyes that made it difficult to tell when he was upset. But this time, there was no doubt. He gently placed his pencil onto his desk, slouched down in his chair, and let out a breath of concession.

I walked over to Russell, wanting to encourage him. Squatting down below his eye level, I asked him what his trouble was.

"I'm stupid," he said.

My heart sank. Even for a young man who had endured so much in such a short life, this was the ultimate white flag of surrender.

I asked him, "What are you passionate about? When the school day is done and you're ready to do something *you* enjoy, what is it?"

He thought for a bit. Then he reversed his slouch, propped himself up a little bit in his chair, and told me his passion was the Volkswagen Beetle. When I asked him to explain it, he started telling me about the motor and every piece, part, and component that made a VW Bug operate. He nearly brought me to tears. Russell was a genius—but he'd never been given a platform for his passion. When asked to prove what

---

5   Individualized Education Plan. For educators, this is a sign that a student has been identified as needing a bit more support. For students, this is often a stamp of inferiority.

he knew, he'd spent nine years, two months, and three weeks doing it in an uncomfortable and often foreign format. Teaching *is* truly an art, but asking Russell to prove what he knew in a way *we* chose stole his imagination's ability and desire to create.

Something had to change. I was *not* going to let his genius be smothered by a traditional approach to assessment. Sure, he needed to learn how to take a test, but I needed to learn how to gather information about what he knew. Yes, he needed help with his math facts, and he had a hard time staying on a line when he was writing a sentence. Sure, he had outbursts when he was trying to read and didn't stay locked into a topic long enough to work through it. But even with those challenges, I knew there had to be a way to help him share his knowledge.

While I would love to tell you I pulled this reflection from the depths of my first year teaching, it's actually from my most recent time as a classroom teacher. Years into teaching, I still wasn't aware of the ramifications of the way I was gathering data about my students. But as I became aware, I started wondering: How many other Russells would thrive if invited and encouraged to share what they know in a comfortable setting?

While we're going to shy away from claiming to serve up the answer to this complicated issue, we will present an option which has worked very well when gathering data for our students: choosing your own assessment.

Choose Your Own Assessment (CYOA)

We teachers often judge the cooks of our classroom solely on the product of their recipe card—without asking them to pick up a spatula. We are relying on one simple form of assessment to gauge the level of proficiency our students have reached on any given standard or objective. To be blunt, it's easier—easier for the teacher to create and monitor, easier to grade, and easier for kids to prepare for. Or so we think.

How often have we completely ruined some of the most delicious meals by eating a couple of buttered popcorn jelly beans[6] or burned the roof of our mouths on a not-quite-done-brownie fresh from the oven? As a kid, we've all been there. As an adult, I'm still guilty of it. Those were certainly not my finest culinary moments.

Similarly, there have been many times I proudly created a lesson, the kids rocked it, and I failed to finish off the "meal" with the proper closure. Rather than riding the momentum of a student-centered classroom, I selfishly funneled all of the unit's energy into a bottle of *yuck*. Yes, I'm talking about the assessment.

My friends know I love making a fool of myself—especially if the foolishness is tied to a grade. Make a music video? You bet. About something we did in class? Even better. Plus, kids love listening to music, right? And YouTube is a great source for students to catch the dance moves that accompany their favorite song. Therefore, I deduced in my sixth year of teaching that it would be a great idea for all my students to create music videos about standards they had learned during Algebra 1. Like we had done so many times before, students would go through the process of changing the lyrics of a song to match a specific topic assigned to them. Once they had the lyrics, choreography was next. After they memorized their lines and their moves, they would record their video and turn it in via flash drive, YouTube—or any other way to show me their outstanding video depicting their knowledge of the standard.

Guadalupe, one of my best academic students, was not pleased. Quiet, introverted, and somewhat of an outlier in a class of outspoken teenagers, she could (and would) solve any math problem put in front of her. She would make a gorgeous slide presentation detailing her level of mastery. She could even write a poem about the quadratic formula! (Crazy, right?). However, for this task, she flat-out refused.

"Mr. Stevens, I'll take the zero. I'm not making a music video."

(Gut punch.)

I was shocked. But I obliged. *If she wants the zero*, I told myself, *I*

---

6 *Blugh. Rakl. Urf.* *gag*

have no option but to put it in the gradebook. Fortunately, my gradebook was set up so zeros didn't destroy a kid's grade, but her choice sticks with me to this day. Sure, the music video was pretty demanding and required a pretty big risk. But Guadalupe wasn't refusing the assignment because of difficulty; she was refusing because I was asking her to go too far outside her comfort zone. She wasn't willing to do it.

In this eye-opening moment, I realized one student's music video was another student's poster, which was another student's computerized slideshow. After this interaction with Guadalupe, I promised myself that when I asked students to prove mastery using a form of expression, I would allow them to choose how they would express it. Although there is no substantive evidence Albert Einstein said the following, it still rings true: "Everybody is a genius. But if you judge a fish by its ability to climb a tree, it will live its whole life believing that it is stupid."[7]

So as our unit on triangle congruency wrapped up, with Guadalupe fresh in my memory, I wanted my students to demonstrate to me they knew—and could explain—how to prove each triangle congruency theorem and CPCTC. Rather than requiring students to raid the poster board section and glitter aisle,[8] I gave them a choice. The assignment:

> Prove you understand the triangle congruence theorems
> in any form of media you choose. If you are using video,
> you may work in groups of no more than three. If you are
> not using video, you will work individually.

With that, on a Wednesday, students worked the entire period to come up with different ways they could prove they knew something. The first few responses were typical of students who had learned how to "play school" for almost a dozen years.

---

7   It's a bummer this quote is used by everyone who wants to criticize the American education system.

8   Have we mentioned that we hate glitter? We do. So please, *please* stop with the glitter. Thanks.

Jinny: We could take a test.

Camilla: We could write a paper.

Sergio: We could say them out loud in front of class.

Mr. Stevens: Yeah, okay, but what else? If this wasn't school, how could you prove to a friend you know something—if you had to *hand* them something?

After two periods, the responses got more interesting. Here's what the students came up with:

Story	Flashcards	Instagram	Instructions	Animation	Twitter
Drawing	Comic Book	Blog	Rap/Song	Pictures	Facebook
Video	Riddles	Poster	Cooking Show	Essay/Novel	Painting
Poem	Article	Live Performance	Speech	Game	Cartoon
Music Video	Collage	Newspaper	Puzzle	Sportscast	Newscast
Slideshow	Presentation	Commercial	Tutorial	Interactive Video	Dating Site
Jokes	Vine				

WOW! Imagine a dating site for triangles!

Are you looking for the love of your life? Have you been identified as a triangle with a specific angle, side, and angle? Well, at TriangleMatch.com, we have the perfect match for you. Come on by, register for your free 180-degree trial, and start making congruency today!

Students' finished projects exceeded all expectations. When Sarah, a student who kept to herself and had a lot more to say in writing than she did using her voice, was given the opportunity to show what she knew in a way she was comfortable with, she chose to create a dreamcatcher. Inside the dreamcatcher were six sets of triangles, each of which highlighted a triangle congruency theorem. On the back of her paper was an explanation of each theorem proof with more details than I could've received through a test.

Another student, Elizabeth, wrote more words on her project than she had said out loud all semester. My issue wasn't her product—it was her process. As I mentioned above, I'd given the kids a day in class to work on their game plan. After that, we moved on, but Elizabeth was distracted. Rather than participating in what we were doing as a class, Elizabeth was drawing. Considering that I was a doodler in school, I always let my students draw in class, as long as it didn't directly interfere with their learning or the learning of students around them.[9] Elizabeth's being a good student let me give her the benefit of the doubt, but my patience was wearing thin. After all, the only thing she was doing in class was drawing anime characters.

Then on the day the project was due, Elizabeth turned in her project—the drawings she had been working on for the past six days. Her entire project was filled with anime characters, each of which included two triangles—each pair representing a different triangle congruence theorem and CPCTC. On the back of each drawing, she had written a small story about who each character was and how the character related to the triangle congruence theorem they were associated with. *Wow!* Thank goodness I hadn't stopped her from drawing so she could tread water with the rest of us!

Plenty of other projects also blew me away. I got my fair share of music videos, musical parodies, and even a few iMovie videos and trailers. Many were outstanding. One video in particular was a death metal music video made by a student who had written the lyrics and music himself. While this makes it sound like I had 175 students and 175 incredible products, quality wasn't the goal of this project. The real value of this project was students demonstrating their knowledge in a way comfortable and effective for them.[10]

---

9 Working in an area with multiple gangs, we had to be aware of what was being "doodled" onto students' papers, binders, body parts, etc.

10 For some of the highlights from our CYOA project in geometry, including all projects mentioned in this section, go to classroomchef.com/CYOA.

EXTRA CREDIT AND EQUITY:
EXTRA CREDIT ONLY FEEDS THE RICH.

If VW-loving Russell had to make a dreamcatcher, draw anime characters, or make a music video, he would have worked with half effort for a few minutes, then given up and spent the next forty minutes—and the next three days—finding something else to occupy himself.[11]

Instead, everyone had the opportunity to prove their knowledge in a way they were comfortable sharing. Russell got the same grade as everyone else, put in a similar amount of work, but took a completely different route. He worked diligently for six consecutive school days, making a flip-book out of white copy paper[12] and a traditional No. 2 pencil.

And here's the cool part: Russell got a one hundred percent. So did Sarah. And so did Elizabeth. The assignment was to prove each of the five triangle congruency theorems and CPCTC, and all three accomplished the goal. When test-taking is the only measure of knowledge, students like Elizabeth and Sarah will likely earned solid Bs on the unit test. Students like Russell will get left behind.

Before beginning the project, it was made clear that absolutely *no extra credit* would be given. The only *extra* kids could receive was getting their work hung in class and posted onto my blog. Okay, there was one bit of extra credit handed out: Each student who turned in their project received a high five as they exited the room. Those who didn't submit anything got a quick conversation with Mr. Stevens after class. Eventually, every single student got a high five and the realization their teacher genuinely cared about them and wanted them to succeed.

---

11 And you ain't gonna like what he does with his time.

12 Also called a "foldable." He made a mini paper book out of a sheet of copy paper.

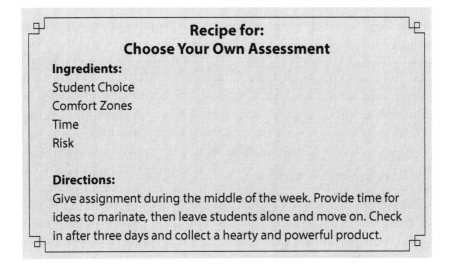

Recipe for:
Choose Your Own Assessment

Ingredients:
Student Choice
Comfort Zones
Time
Risk

Directions:
Give assignment during the middle of the week. Provide time for ideas to marinate, then leave students alone and move on. Check in after three days and collect a hearty and powerful product.

A STEP IN THE RIGHT DIRECTION

I learned from doing this type of assessment students will work as hard as they can when given the freedom to do so. In fact, truth be told, some students bit off a little more than they could chew. Angelica was going to create a website with all kinds of cool features on it. But her mom and dad got into a big argument, and her dad left the house. Suddenly, Angelica's focus was on comforting her mom and being there for the family. She simply didn't have the time or mental energy to invest in a major project.

Because I knew she wanted to create a website and was willing to help, I kept asking her about it until she relented and told me the reason for her change in plans. We decided a website was too much to take on at that time, and she settled for a foldable which she colored, cut, and turned in with a reluctant smile on her face. She was happy with it, but felt she had let *me* down because it wasn't what she set out to do. Maybe it wasn't her original plan, but Angelica turned in a completed project she could proudly put her name on.

The lesson here is this: Life happens, and we need to be far more flexible to support our students during those bumps in the road.

Interestingly—and incredibly rewarding—no student judged the other projects or felt theirs deserved more credit. No one asked why Elizabeth earned *academic* points for her *creative* time. While we may not have the perfect answer for assessments yet, allowing students to decide how to prove their knowledge is one helluva step in the right direction.

SHOW YOUR KNOWLEDGE

While working with a group of K-8 teachers in Northern California, we challenged them to show what they learned; in short, Choose Your Own Assessment. Given fifteen minutes, teachers were to work in groups (or individually) to create something to prove what they had learned during our workshop, and then share it with the room. With no other guidance, they buried themselves in their projects, scrambling to come up with a product they were proud to share. Most of the attendees stuck to what was comfortable, but a few took a risk and tried tools we'd mentioned during the previous five hours.

Teachers created Padlet walls, Google Slides, Prezis—even a paper foldable to demonstrate their learning. Some created art from nothing—writing a poem or shooting a quick video. Others cleverly arranged the items on their table into a collage. Others tackled a *twofer*, addressing our prompt *and* giving them material for an upcoming class. They created a "Would You Rather?" task, wrote a Desmos activity, or designed a "Which One Doesn't Belong?" task, all of which would fit nicely into the upcoming lessons or units.

As we walked around the room to listen to their conversations, we were jazzed to see adults tapping into childlike excitement. If we asked everyone to make a poster, some would've been uncomfortable—and much less enthusiastic. In fact, most would have mentally checked out.

How many "poster share-outs" have you done in *your* career?[13] And yes, it's strange to think that teachers wouldn't feel comfortable standing

---

13 If you work at the district level, probably north of a dozen. How many of them are still hanging anywhere? We'd wager zero.

up and talking—until we remember the stakes are raised when they're among peers presenting outside of their comfort zones.[14]

The same goes for our students.

TIME: TRY LESS OF IT

When students did this CYOA to prove triangle congruence, they were given five days. When K-8 teachers did this in a full-day workshop, they were given only fifteen minutes. If they had been given two days, we would have received some pretty good products, some decent ones, and then a handful of "meh, I ran out of time" products. The most significant "shoulda" we took from the original CYOA for triangles was "shoulda given the students *less* time."

Jon Corippo, CUE's Director of Academic Innovation,[15] talks about getting students out of "The Suck," a term that describes the window of time during a project when students drag their feet, knowing they have time to accomplish it later. (See the dashed line below.)

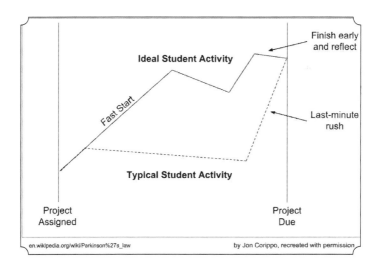

en.wikipedia.org/wiki/Parkinson%27s_law   by Jon Corippo, recreated with permission

---

14 If you have the chance, read about intellectual autonomy on Robert's blog at robertkaplinsky.com.

15 As of this writing, Jon still works for CUE. The guy changes high-level jobs like he's test-driving BMWs.

We've all been there—probably more than once.[16] If you give students a week to complete a project, most start on day four.

Instead of giving students *more* time to produce a better product, defeating The Suck encourages teachers to give *less* time to get a better product. In fifteen minutes, our group of teachers produced some amazing things and were inspired to continue working past the deadline to refine their materials. We firmly believe, along with Mr. Corippo, students will do the same.

Think about how you gather information about what students have learned. How can *you* do something student-centered in your classroom to allow students the freedom to prove what they know? And what would they do if they got to choose what's comfortable for them? Capture your thoughts on the recipe card at classroomchef.com/recipecard, and then share them with someone at your site, in your department—or the world.

---

16 And every week in grad school.

THE BILL

Let's talk about the cost.

Matt's wife loves cooking shows—*Top Chef, Chopped,* even *Shark Tank* episodes where a gourmet cupcake startup is asking for an investor. As a result of his wife's enthusiasm about foodie fame, the Vaudreys now save up all year for a fancy (aka *expensive*) anniversary meal at a celebrity chef's restaurant—that Matt researches well in advance. As you can imagine, the bill for these fancy six-course dinners runs about ten times the cost of an average dinner out—pretty steep for a teacher and a youth pastor with three kids.

In the classroom, however, the only real cost is *risk*.

Model risk by trying new lessons; show students that you'll deviate from what's comfortable.

Model risk by showing vulnerability. When students ask how many monomial cubes are in the bag, take a risk by saying out loud, "I don't know. Let's find out."

Model risk by encouraging guesses.[1] More importantly, make your class a place where the cost of risk is low and the expectation is high, like Ms. Webb's class.

---

1 "When we say to students, 'Don't be afraid to be wrong,' we better be damn sure they can take that risk with *zero* penalties." —Fawn Nguyen

CHAPTER 16
RISKS AND REWARDS

(Matt) met Kelli Webb during the first month of my first year teaching.

I don't actually recall the exact day I met her. My first two weeks teaching were such a whirlwind—the details bleed together into a trauma of botched activities, stuttering lessons, clunky worksheets, and the occasional discipline issue—which soon became frequent discipline issues. I do, however, remember when I first saw Ms. Webb's fifth period. My assistant principal—after watching the kitchen nightmare that was *my* fifth period—said, "You should watch Kelli teach. I'll get you a sub." During my planning period the next day, I followed the A.P. to Kelli's classroom with my notebook in hand, completely clueless about what I would write down.

I wish I had videotaped it. It was pure poetry—like watching Olympic figure skating.

First, the students filed in with subdued murmurs and sat down quietly. I had seen these students during lunch—they were not quiet people. Ms. Webb taught algebra readiness, an eighth-grade class for students who hadn't passed pre-algebra the year before. They were a rough-and-rowdy bunch of surly teens with odors and attitudes sour enough to curdle the milk in your gramma's teacup. This wasn't even my class, and I got nervous.

"Please take out your packet and turn to S.P. 15." Ms. Webb calmly spoke over the rustle of paper. The bell had just sounded and all her students were in their seats, most with their pencils out. I looked around the room and thought I was dreaming:

Her eighteen students were evenly spread throughout the room, most of them alone at a table.

All the hats were off.

Nobody touched anybody else.

No backpacks or purses were in laps; all rested on the floor or on a chair next to them.

Most of the students had their packets out and were hunched over them, silently working.

Ms. Webb began to weave through the rows, giving little comments. "Thank you for getting started, Jamal." "Good start, Maria. Put your mirror away, please."

And *this* was when I knew I was in the presence of greatness: "Miguel, please spit out your gum."

Miguel curled his lip, "I don't have any gum."

"Let me tell you what I don't do." Ms. Webb bristled, straightening to her full six-foot-two and narrowing her eyes. "I don't argue with children. Spit it out."

Miguel paused, considering his chances of winning a battle with a woman twice his size and thrice his age. He wisely stood and leaned over the trashcan as Ms. Webb moved on to other tables. The *thunk* of his gum in the metal wastebasket was the only noise in room A5, save for the delicate scratch of pencil on paper.

After about five minutes, Ms. Webb produced some more magic. She went through the worksheet with the class. Now, any teacher can walk through problems, but nobody in Ms. Webb's class got bored. She pulled names from a cup of popsicle sticks (what teachers called "random sampling" in those days) and asked students for their responses.

Ms. Webb: Ysela, number five.

Ysela: Umm...I didn't get it.

Ms. Webb: Okay, what do you think we should do first?

Ysela: Umm…Take away seven?

Ms. Webb (grimaces): Ooh! Is there a mathematical way to say that?

Ysela: Umm…Subtract seven from both sides of the equation.

Ms. Webb: Oh, much better. I like that. Damon, take over number five.

She was magical. She coaxed responses from students who hated (or at least bragged about hating) math—the ones who have made a career out of coasting and doing nothing. But they have nowhere to hide from the watchful eye of Ms. Webb.

And nowhere to hide from taking a risk.

Non-teachers may not realize this, but Ysela was hoping to be ignored, skipped, and left in peace to text under her desk and do her

IF YOU DON'T KNOW THE ANSWER, TAKE A GUESS. TAKE A RISK.

makeup. Getting students like Ysela to take a stab at a problem is hard work. By eighth grade, she'd learned that the three magic words "I don't know" would get teachers to skip over her in most other classes. Enough skips would get her ignored entirely. In Ms. Webb's class, though, there were no ignored seats, no back of the class, no hats pulled down, and no students getting to pass on a problem.

The lesson (one of many) I took from Ms. Webb's class: If you don't know the answer, take a guess.

Take a risk.

MODEL RISK—IT'S WORTH IT

Right now, I (Matt) am preparing to give a demonstration lesson featuring Desmos and Barbie Bungee to algebra and pre-calculus students in a district where I've never taught math. It's a little terrifying—and

I'm giddy about it. While it is true that classrooms are unforgiving places to learn to teach, the stakes are really low if your students like you.[1] Here's how it looks:

You try a risky lesson. It goes okay.

You give a regular lesson. Students are more interested in your style because you tried something risky.

You try a riskier lesson. It goes okay. Students are *more* interested in your risky lessons.

You try a still riskier lesson. It goes *awfully terribly horrible and ends in a fireball engulfing the village.*

You give three days of regular, *safe* lessons in a row, and a student asks, "Can we do something fun today?"

Your students prefer risky lessons, even if they fail spectacularly. A fantastic belly flop is still better than stepping down the ladder into the shallow end for 180 days in a row.

You'll be easily forgiven by students, because your risk usually pays off, even if a few lessons don't. Administrators and parents are equally forgiving of bombed lessons when the good ones pay off.

Let's be clear: Trying to create five-star learning experiences can be a scary way to teach. While teaching the traditional way, like fast food,

> ## WHILE TEACHING THE TRADITIONAL WAY, LIKE FAST FOOD, IS EASY AND CONSISTENT, IT'S ALSO UNINSPIRING.

is easy and consistent, it's also uninspiring. Your students deserve better than a traditional education. And you, the educator, can give them that.

When John and I were students, the two jobs of the teacher were to deliver instruction and check answers. With websites like Khan

---

1 Pam Grossman, cited by Dan Meyer, "Two Weeks Later," May 20, 2011, http://blog. mrmeyer.com/2011/anyqs-two-weeks-later.

Academy and apps like PhotoMath, the teacher of the nineties can be replaced by a free website and a two-dollar app. Sir Arthur C. Clarke, author of *2001: A Space Odyssey*, once said, "A teacher who can be replaced by a machine *should* be." The fast food teacher isn't just boring, she's fast becoming obsolete.

The phrase "be a good example" gets tossed around a lot, and it's as tired as many of the aging Sunday school teachers who use it. However, there's truth there; as the teacher, you have dozens of students looking to you every day. When you model risk-taking, students begin to mimic what you do. And it looks pretty cool.

Sack Full of Monomial Cubes

My students had just finished fifth-period Algebra and were about to start sixth period Math Support. They were placed in this double period of math by the office to support them in their "academic need," since they hadn't been successful in math prior to eighth grade. I knew before they stared back at me at 2:25 p.m. that they would not be as excited as I was to review "like terms" using a foldable and some guided practice. I'd planned to use the monomial cubes[2] to do some random practice with combining like terms.

We never even got that far. I held up the bag and immediately, a student asked, "How many dice are in the bag?"

Oooh. I thought. *This just got much more interesting.* "I dunno. I made them a while ago. How many do you think are in the bag?"

A couple students called out guesses before someone yelled, "Can we see one of them?"

We polled the class for a few guesses (where the median was about sixty-five) before writing down our "Too High" guess, our "Too Low" guess, and our estimate.[3] Then we started counting them together.

---

2 Imagine dice, but with a different "monomial" on each side, like 3x, -9, or $10x^2$.

3 We can't recall if it was Dan Meyer or Andrew Stadel who started this line of mathematical guessing, but in either case, we like it and use it often.

We were several months into the school year, so it was normal for a student to call out suggestions: "Is there an easier way to group them for counting? Those piles are confusing me."

"How would you like to group them? Come show me."

Ramiro strolled to the front and lined them up in five-by-five groups, leaving one leftover.

"Ah, okay, five by five...so we've got three twenty-fives plus one, so..." (Wait for students to think...five Mississippi...six Mississippi...)

Victor yelled, "Seventy-six! I was close!"

Dylan was ticked. His guess of ninety wasn't as close as Adriana, who had seventy-five.

There were six-and-a-half minutes before the "Clean-Up Song" began to play, plenty of time for some more estimations and guesses. So I posed this question (which I stole from my mom, who attended middle school in the seventies): "What if we were on a planet where humans had four fingers on each hand instead of five?" My students paused and thought for a little bit. Then Dylan came to the front and re-arranged the stacks into five grids of four by four, one of which was hollow—missing a few cubes.

"Hey! Five sixteens with four missing!" I cheered. "That's also seventy-six!"

Yeah. It was a good day.

A Great Time to Be a Teacher

When we started teaching and wanted advice, we went door-to-door in our building. The result was a mixed bag of advice—both good and bad.

For example, during my (Matt's) first year of teaching, a fellow math teacher bragged, "I'm so glad I took on a student teacher; I don't have to do *anything* in my class these days. I can go online and research remote control cars."[4] The same year, a teacher on his team offered great advice on recording scores, which Matt still uses today.

Teachers love talking about teaching; bad teachers love talking about bad teaching. As new teachers, we didn't know whose advice was helpful and whose was jaded and disillusioned.

Today, we don't have to go door-to-door. We can ask questions online and receive answers from teachers around the world—and just as easily, we can weed out the good answers from the bad. What a great time to be a teacher! The tools to improve our skills are widely used and easily accessible. Take Twitter, for example:

Matt Vaudrey
@MrVaudrey

Am I crazy for trying to teach slope to 8th graders as Δy/Δx? We describe vertical change and horizontal change. #mathchat #msmathchat

LIKES
2

7:18 AM - 15 Jan 2014

Within twenty-four hours, I received nearly fifty responses, many of which went deep into the mechanics of slope and education. Some highlights appear on the next page.

---

4 Six years later, I saw this teacher at a conference where I was presenting. We were both much better at our jobs.

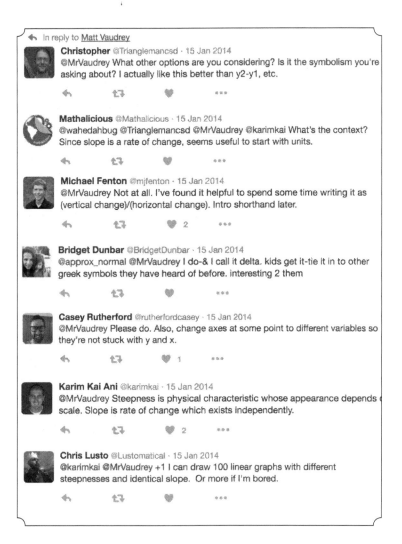

In reply to Matt Vaudrey

Christopher @Trianglemancsd · 15 Jan 2014
@MrVaudrey What other options are you considering? Is it the symbolism you're asking about? I actually like this better than y2-y1, etc.

Mathalicious @Mathalicious · 15 Jan 2014
@wahedahbug @Trianglemancsd @MrVaudrey @karimkai What's the context? Since slope is a rate of change, seems useful to start with units.

Michael Fenton @mjfenton · 15 Jan 2014
@MrVaudrey Not at all. I've found it helpful to spend some time writing it as (vertical change)/(horizontal change). Intro shorthand later.

♥ 2

Bridget Dunbar @BridgetDunbar · 15 Jan 2014
@approx_normal @MrVaudrey I do-& I call it delta. kids get it-tie it in to other greek symbols they have heard of before. interesting 2 them

Casey Rutherford @rutherfordcasey · 15 Jan 2014
@MrVaudrey Please do. Also, change axes at some point to different variables so they're not stuck with y and x.

♥ 1

Karim Kai Ani @karimkai · 15 Jan 2014
@MrVaudrey Steepness is physical characteristic whose appearance depends on scale. Slope is rate of change which exists independently.

♥ 2

Chris Lusto @Lustomatical · 15 Jan 2014
@karimkai @MrVaudrey +1 I can draw 100 linear graphs with different steepnesses and identical slope. Or more if I'm bored.

In the conversation above, I posed a new-teacher-level question about teaching slope.[5] What followed was better than the best teacher's lounge conversation I've had and better than any department meeting. Teachers from all over offered their opinions on how I should teach *my* class. Twitter gives me access to a staff lounge spanning the world— where no question is too silly, and most teachers are kind and helpful to others seeking to grow. If you're nervous about a lesson, a subject, or *anything* related to teaching, ask for input on Twitter first.[6] It's free, and you'll get real feedback from math teachers who want to improve one another's craft.[7]

You have the most rewarding job on the planet, and you have all the necessary ingredients to excel. (And most of them are free!) You also have a team of students, parents, and administrators who will likely be excited to join you as you explore new and interesting ways to provide learning opportunities for kids. Plus, you have a whole kitchen full of talented chefs online waiting to share their expertise with you—and to improve their craft alongside you.

So what are you waiting for? Start experimenting in your classroom. You'll see your students get excited about coming back for more. And, if they hate a particular lesson, they will let you know. Use their feedback to adjust your recipe.

In the next chapter, we'll share how you can improve your results— and show your students you value their opinions—by asking for honest reviews.

---

5   I should note that I'd taught slope several times before. You're never too seasoned to learn something new.

6   The aforementioned Dan Meyer writes about this here: Meyer, "Pretending Closed Questions Are Open," November 29, 2011, http://blog.mrmeyer.com/2011/pretending-closed-questions-are-open.

7   If we haven't emphasized this yet, go check out the #MTBoS hashtag on Twitter. The mercifully abbreviated "Math-Twitter-Blogosphere" is full of other math teachers who like improving and sharing.

THE REVIEWS

We stay at the Hampton Inn most of the time we travel. After each stay, we get an email asking for our feedback—on *everything*. How were the sheets? Was the breakfast hot enough? Did the front desk have a sheen from too many elbows resting on it? Did your room key work? How about the night manager? Did he smell okay? Was the ad in the elevator smug, yet tasteful? Were there enough channels to watch the news in Korean?

Hampton Inn—and much of the business world—knows the people most qualified to review a product are the ones receiving it.

So why don't teachers ask their *students* about class?

The cooks in a restaurant kitchen are not graded by one another. Sure, their boss is going to assess their cleanliness in the kitchen, their efficiency, their ability to work with the team, and a myriad of other criteria. And yes, plenty of cooks get fired because of their reputation among colleagues. However, the measure of the cook isn't based on her peers' ratings. Her value is determined by the customers. Because of that, we have Yelp.com—the greatest and most volatile culinary review website ever created.

Yelp gives *everyone* the ability to offer opinions about the service, pricing, and quality of food at restaurants all over the world. When we travel to a new part of the country, we can either hit up the safe chain restaurants like Applebee's or Burger King, or we use Yelp ratings to help us select some local fare.

We choose Yelp.

No doubt, there will be a review from an isolated, terrible experience—usually from a customer who has an axe to grind with the waiter. Sure, we read those, but a single bad review won't deter us when the majority of customers have had a positive culinary experience.

For better or for worse, students don't have the opportunity to choose their teachers. Sure, a few special circumstances exist, but more often than not, kids are stuck with the teachers to whom they're assigned on day one. And to think, many teachers go through the entire 180 days of teaching without ever seeking a review from their customers.

CHAPTER 17
THE TEACHER REPORT CARD

We knew we'd be good friends and colleagues when we discovered we'd both[1] implemented a semi-annual "Grade the Teacher" segment in our classes. We wanted our teaching compasses pointed toward true north; we wanted to be sure our kids were getting the experience we thought—*hoped*—we were delivering.

At the end of every grading period, we gave students the opportunity to grade us. Submissions were anonymous, so the students could be as honest as they wanted when responding. The Teacher Report Card gets feedback from the people we see every single day as a way to get better at what we do.

It's Yelp for the classroom.

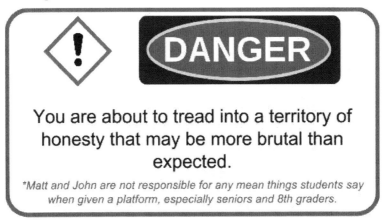

! DANGER

You are about to tread into a territory of honesty that may be more brutal than expected.

Matt and John are not responsible for any mean things students say when given a platform, especially seniors and 8th graders.

---

1 Separately. Before we met each other.

We were fearless in our questions, asking students to rank us on a scale of one to five (or a grade of "A" to "F"). We chose questions specifically designed to give us the most meaningful feedback. For example, does the teacher:

- Respect each student?

- Try to see students' point of view?

- Make me feel important?

- Treat me as an individual?

These and many other questions extracted some real—oftentimes painful—flaws in our teaching. Unfortunately, we weren't (and still aren't) perfect at our jobs. Fortunately, we were okay with that and were willing to improve. However, our students also knew we liked to ask them questions and give them an opportunity to teach *us* a few things. After all, *they're* the ones who get to spend 180 days with us, and they certainly had some opinions on where we need to improve. We got some fantastic responses and good data from their responses to questions like:

- What do you like BEST about this class?

- How can this class be improved?

- Your friend tells you they have Mr. _____ as their teacher next year. What do you tell them?

- Sometimes, the teacher _____, but not always.

- Sometimes, the teacher lets the class _____, but not always.[2]

Unflinching vulnerability reveals two things to students: first, we are serious about improving as teachers, and second, our students' opinions *matter* to us.

---

2 Classroom management is built on consistency. These two questions revealed some clear chinks in our armor.

Once the students had completed the survey, the data was ours to keep, and we were free to choose what we did with it. It wouldn't end up on any formal evaluation, probably wouldn't come up in staff lounge conversation, and certainly wouldn't get discussed in front of the class. The insights we collected were for us to use to improve at the profession we love.[3]

John's Report Card Analysis for 2013

Before I (John) share the good, the bad, and the ugly, the math nerd in me needs to quantify the numeric responses. Each response was on a scale of one to five, five being the best. My top five categories were:

Seems to enjoy teaching	4.69
Respects each student	4.65
Speaks clearly	4.65
Dresses professionally	4.65
Encourages me to be responsible	4.56

I liked that these were my top five. I was happy to know my message was interpreted correctly, loud and clear: *I will respect each and every one of you to the best of my abilities.* Because I had a lot of English language learners and had been accused of talking too fast, I was glad to see I was apparently learning to speak more clearly. One of my biggest hopes was for my love of teaching to come through in my lessons, and it certainly must have for my students to rate this the highest on the list. I dressed professionally—slacks, long-sleeve dress shirt, and a tie—four days a week. No, it wasn't going to create better test scores. Likely, it didn't make any difference at all. But I believe my attire set the tone—for my students and me—that the classroom was a professional

---

3 And we share it with you, in the name of *unflinching vulnerability*. John's is printed in this chapter, and Matt's is at mrvaudrey.com/reportcard13.

environment, and we would conduct business as such (while having fun, of course).[4]

And while I'd love to talk only about the top five, not everything can be great. Here are my bottom five:

Makes me feel important	3.87
Shows interest in students' lives	4.07
Gives good, fair assignments	4.16
Has interesting lessons	4.16
Encourages different opinions	4.18

Honestly, these stung a little. While I admit my mind had been elsewhere the previous few weeks with a new job, new house, and new area to research, the time I'd spent in class was supposed to be dedicated to the seventy-eight eyeballs looking at me—and the thirty-nine brains and hearts which showed up to be exercised, nurtured, and grown—every period. Clearly, no matter how much I wanted to think I was getting through, I wasn't. I've never been okay with a "C+."

A 3.87 out of 5 equates to a 77.4 percent—a tough pill to swallow. With so many students, showing interest in each of their lives was tough, but it was something I clearly needed to improve. Giving good and fair assessment was partially the nature of the beast known as Algebra 1. At the same time, I didn't want to use it as an excuse and knew it would get better the next year. Interesting lessons? You mean algebra isn't interesting? I'd accept an 83.2 percent there for the sake of not losing my sanity over trying to make systems of equations the most entertaining work they'd ever done. The final one cut me a little, considering I tried to get different opinions. While I knew I had some work to do, I appreciated their honesty and was glad I'd asked for their feedback.

---

4 *Preparing the Kitchen* from Part 1.

After the numeric ratings, I gave a loaded "opinion rifle" to the students and let them take aim—at me—by asking, "How can this class be improved?" The responses ranged from helpful to downright ugly.

"Let us have snacks. Use the videos on your website more often."

Snacks, no. School rule. The website comment was a good one though!

"You could use more colors around the classroom."

This response came up more than once, duly noted. I'm a stereotypical jock dude and a math teacher. We tend not to be on the creative side of any creativity spectrum. I'll work on it.

"The class can be improved by never doing the serpinskis [sic] triangle ever again, poor children."[5]

Bwahahahaha!

"This class can be improved by treating every student equally and not having favorites."

Eeeesh. Totally what I didn't want to happen, but it's inevitable, I guess. It's painful to think I'm perceived as having favorites. The bad part is that there were a couple like this. I know that it's not my job to get every student to like me. At the same time, I try to feed off the energy of the class, which can be misconstrued as favoring the kids who bring the most energy.

Thankfully, they had plenty of good to report when I asked, "What do you like best about the class?"[6]

"What I like best about this class is that everything is fair for each and every one of the students no matter who you are."

In light of the "favorites" comment in the "needs improvement" section, I had to share this one with you.

"The thing I like best about his class is that he makes difficult things easy."

---

5   This is a project we did at the end of testing every year. Students were tasked with drawing a perfect Sierpinski Triangle down to 1/8" triangles. It's incredibly difficult, yet teaches students about precision and perseverance and, no matter how smart they are, how to deal with failure.

6   All responses were copied and pasted from the actual survey.

"The fact that Mr. Stevens gives us the trust and ability to be creative."

"I liked how all the lessons we learned were taught to us in simple terms, but it didn't sound like he was teaching preschool. He treated us like young men and women."

"I like how Mr. Stevens does his best to improve everything. He likes to be perfect and make his students happy. He's a really cool teacher to have. His class was a great experience. Hopefully his next students love him as much as we do."

And because any good survey leaves room for additional comments, I asked, "Is there anything else you'd like to add?" This response was one of my favorites:[7]

"I want to say that I am honored to be one of your students for the 2012–2013 school year. I hope you have an amazing summer and enjoy your job at your new school. I will miss you and hope to see you again in the future! And thank you for everything you have taught me."

---

7 The response, not the student. The student remained anonymous. But I'd high-five him/her if I knew who it was.

A Take-Home Container, Please!

In this book, we have described in depth the things we like the most about the math classes that we've seen. It's quite possible that you have an example from your class that looks nothing like the examples given in these pages.

It's also possible—even likely—that you disagree with some of the points in his book.

In fact, we *hope* you are skeptical.

If you disagree, we hope you will not keep it to yourself. If you disagree, do so loudly, often, and in conversation with other educators. Find us and let us know where you think we're missing the point. It would be the height of arrogance for us to assume that we've arrived at the perfect way to teach all students.

Education—by its very nature—is imperfect, diverse, and requires master teachers to make real-time adjustments on a daily basis.

All lesson planning models, including the one you just read, will not work perfectly for every student.

Whether or not you disagreed with the point of this book, we can all agree on one thing: **Math education is always evolving.**

Indeed, when we look back on this book in ten or twenty years, we will likely wince at the dated instructional strategies.

We remain confident, however, that all teachers—past, present, and future—must take dynamic risks for the sake of their students.

At the very least, educators must be regularly asking themselves big questions about education:

- How will my students respond to this topic?
- How can I connect this topic for this skill to the world at large?
- What kind of adults do I hope to create by building this skill in my students?
- What is the purpose of my math class?

It is no longer enough to teach the textbook and hope that their teacher *next* year will fill in the gaps. That kind of disconnected, uninspired teaching has made math the class most despised by adults. Some math classes are so pointless and boring that grown men and women will say with a straight face, "I'm not a math person."[1]

But math classes aren't the only ones that make students struggle. What about the student who took three years of German, but can only ask for a beer and directions to the bathroom? And forget foreign languages, what about *English*? Students have four years of high school English, but do they know the difference between preterit verbs and past progressive verbs? We just did a Google search on the terms, and we're still fuzzy. Other classes—not just math—are in need of change, and *you* can be the catalyst for that change.

Make every class meaningful.

Make *learning* meaningful.

Education is a worthy profession. We teachers are charged with the mission of preparing the next generation of citizens for their place in society. To that end, nothing but excellence will do. And ironically, to become excellent, you'll need to fail.

A lot.

---

1 Truly, it's just unfair. Zero parents will tell teachers, "Oh, I'm not surprised she's struggling with English; I'm illiterate. I was never a book person in school."

You'll need to stay up late and work on weekends preparing a lesson, only to have it go so badly that you scrap it halfway into class. Some lessons will leave your students more confused than they were before it started; the *really* bad ones will make students say *to your face* during class, "I'm more confused than when we started."

It will be okay. Keep trying.

Only by trying and failing can you find ways to hone your craft and become a master of your classroom kitchen. Only in failure are we driven to grow. And in really big failure, we learn really big lessons.

Hopefully, somewhere in these pages, you saw something that would be a risk for you to try.

Yes, you might fail.

Then pick yourself up—take what you learned—and make learning meaningful.

Become a Classroom Chef.

~John and Matt

For more resources, visit ClassroomChef.com.

THE PANTRY

Secret Ingredients
(a.k.a. Works Cited)

Chapter 2

Zach de la Rocha, Garth Richardson, "Know Your Enemy," Rage Against the Machine, *Rage Against the Machine*, Epic Records, 1992.

Dan Meyer, "If Math Is the Aspirin, How Do You Create The Headache?", *Mr. Meyer* (blog), June 17, 2015, http://blog.mrmeyer.com/2015/if-math-is-the-aspirin-then-how-do-you-create-the-headache/.

Robert Burns, "To a Mouse" Poems, Chiefly in the Scottish Dialect, 1786.

Chapter 3

"Teacher Attrition Costs United States up to $2.2 Billion Annually Says New Alliance Report," Alliance for Excellent Education press release, July 17, 2014, http://all4ed.org/press/teacher-attrition-costs-united-states-up-to-2-2-billion-annually-says-new-alliance-report/.

Harry K. and Rosemary T. Wong, *The First Days of School: How to Be an Effective Teacher* (Mountain View, CA: Harry K. Wong Publications, Inc., 2009), 111.

Sun Tzu, *The Art of War*, trans. Lionel Giles (London: n.p., 1910), n.p.

Chip and Dan Heath, *Switch: How to Change Things When Change Is Hard* (New York: Broadway Books, 2010), n.p.

CHAPTER 6

Dan Meyer "Math Class Needs a Makeover," *TED Talk*, May 2010, accessed February 24, 2016, https://www.ted.com/talks/dan_meyer_math_curriculum_makeover/transcript?language=en.

CHAPTER 7

Albert Einstein and Leopold Infield, The Evolution of Physics (New York: Simon and Schuster, 1938), p. 95.

CHAPTER 9

Carcharodon Megalodon, from Wikimedia Commons, accessed February 24, 2016, https://commons.wikimedia.org/wiki/File:Carcharodon_megalodon.jpg.

South Florida Shark Club, accessed February 24, 2016, http://southfloridasharkclub.com/foro/viewtopic.php?p=14519.

Mountain Megalodons, accessed February 24, 2016, mountain-megalodons.com/monster.html.

Parzi, Megalodon Tooth with Two Great White Shark Teeth, from Wikimedia Commons, April 12, 2012, https://commons.wikimedia.org/wiki/File:Megalodon_tooth_with_great_white_sharks_teeth-3.jpg.

Scarlet23, Megalodon Scale, Wikimedia Commons, March 8, 2013, SVG file, https://commons.wikimedia.org/wiki/File:Megalodon_scale.svg.

CHAPTER 11

Graham Fletcher, "The Cookie Monster," Questioning My Metacognition (blog), gfletchy.com/the-cookie-monster/.

Jamie Duncan, "A First Grade Teacher Enters the Math World," Elementary Math Addict (blog), August 16, 2015, elementary-mathaddict.com/2015/08/a-first-grade-teacher-enters-math-world.html.

Duncan, "Notice Wonder Meets Numberless Word," November 22, 2015, elementarymathaddict.com/2015/11/notice-wonder-meets-numberless-word.html.

CHAPTER 12

"Mathematical Modeling with Exponential and Logarithmic Functions," *The Monterey Institute for Technology and Education*, accessed February 24, 2016, montereyinstitute.org/courses/DevelopmentalMath/COURSE_TEXT2_RESOURCE/U18_L4_T2_text_final.html.

Andrew Stadel, "Thank You Math Mistakes," *Divisible by 3* (blog), April 16, 2013, http://mr-stadel.blogspot.com/2013/04/thank-you-math-mistakes.html.

CHAPTER 13

Simon Pegg, *Good Reads*, accessed February 24, 2016, goodreads.com/quotes/556142-being-a-geek-is-all-about-being-honest-about-what.

CHAPTER 14

Kathleen McIntosh, "Science Sampler: Potato Candle," *National Science Teachers Association*, accessed February 24, 2016, https://learningcenter.nsta.org/product_detail.aspx?id=10.2505/4/ss03_027_01_44.

Mary Bourassa, "MPM2D - Day 49: Candy Lab & Chocolate Milk," *M^3 (Making Math Meaningful* (blog), November 19, 2015, http://marybourassa.blogspot.com/2015/11/mpm2d-day-49-candy-lab-chocolate-milk.html.

Chapter 15

Malcolm Gladwell, "Malcolm Gladwell – Zeitgeist Americas 2013," *YouTube* video, September 16, 2013, youtube.com/watch?v=3UEwbRWFZVc.

"Theorems for Congruent Triangles," *Oswego City School District Regents Exam Prep Center*, accessed February 24, 2016, regentsprep.org/regents/math/geometry/gp4/ltriangles.htm.

Jon Corippo. "Avoiding 'the suck' for Project Based Schools," *SlideShare* presentation, August 10, 2011, slideshare.net/jcorippo/avoiding-the-suck-for-project-based-schools.

The Bill

Fawn Nguyen, Twitter post, February 20, 2016, 9:27 a.m., https://twitter.com/fawnpnguyen/status/697471848846487552.

Chapter 16

Pam Grossman, cited by Dan Meyer, "Two Weeks Later," May 20, 2011, http://blog.mrmeyer.com/2011/anyqs-two-weeks-later.

Arthur C. Clarke, "Electronic Tutors," Omni Magazine, June 1980, n.p.

Appendix A
Chefs Who Inspire Us

Every great chef is inspired by the work of other chefs. Bobby Flay wouldn't be "Bobby Flay" without the work of great chefs who came before him. And how many other chefs likely gave Lorraine Pascale the push she needed to accomplish the incredible work she has done? But we're not talking about the famous *As Seen On TV* chefs. Think about John's grandfather, Dede, the Macedonian immigrant with a third-grade education, who worked his way up to owning his own restaurant. He and countless others like him worked hard and overcame obstacles to become *great* at their craft.

Throughout the process of writing this book, *and* long before it, we have become connected with many incredible educators around the world and from all content areas. In fact, we could write a book just describing why you should connect with people who will push you to be better. But for the sake of keeping this reasonable, we have created a *Top Chefs* list of educators who push us to be better. Our hope here is that you actively seek them out, ask them questions, allow them to push you to be better—and push them back in return. After all, as a few close friends say, we're #BetterTogether.

These lists are not exclusive, nor are they highlight reels. Rather, they are a launch pad for your use to leverage the knowledge of their educational kitchens to be helpful in your own classroom. Oh, and tell 'em John and Matt sent you via @ClassroomChef. That might help!

The handle *@ClassroomChef* has "lists" divided by content or idea—a great place to start if you're new to Twitter and want to find new voices to advise you.

twitter.com/classroomchef/lists

APPENDIX B
SALAD BAR OF FAVORITES

During the course of our careers as math teachers, we've built up an arsenal of great ideas, thanks in large part to the growing community on Twitter self-identified as #MTBoS (Math Twitter Blog-o-Sphere). This section showcases some of our palatable, ready-to-use favorite resources for use in your classroom.

For our favorites, head to ClassroomChef.com/links.

ACKNOWLEDGMENTS

JOHN

Taking big risks often means making big sacrifices, and none of this would be possible without the love and support of Erin, Luke, and Nolan. Everything I do is to provide the best possible life for my family, and I am forever grateful for your unwavering support. Thank you.

A young and naïve me never would've made it out of my first two years without Mandy Janssen, my mentor and confidante for when things really went haywire (which felt like, well, every day). While my content knowledge was there, it was obvious that I had zero teaching experience, was hired on an emergency credential, and was more worried about being a mentor than a good teacher. You found a way to make me a better version of myself.

It's funny how some things turn out by accident. I joined Twitter to engage in public banter with my brother, never imagining that there was a world of supportive math teachers who were ready and able to help me get through the toughest times I faced as an educator. For that, and many other questionable decisions you've helped me make over the years, I thank you, Matthew. Mom and Dad, you're in on that as well. Thank you for always being there for us. I love you.

While on Twitter, it was Jon Corippo who saved my career, asking for a teacher to come work for him. I was at a crossroads of leaving education or trying something new, and he provided that spark. Although I didn't take that giant leap to join Obi-Wan Corippo, he encouraged me (and still does) to take risks. The world is a better place with you in it, Jon.

This little community of math teachers we have copiously referenced, the #MTBoS, has provided a safe space on Twitter to be wrong, get help, and get better. From the ridiculous conversations and friendly heckling to the digital shoulder to lean on, this group epitomizes the staff lounge. When I have a question, need help improving something, or need a safe space to be wrong, this group on Twitter is the first place I turn to. You keep the creative wheels spinning, and I thank you so much for that.

Dave and Shelley reached out to Matt and me to write a book, otherwise these words probably would have never found their way onto this page. You invested in us and we are indebted to you for the faith you have shown. Here's to hoping that it's only the beginning of supporting teachers who want to do what is best for kids.

MATT

To my little family, Pumpkin, Pickle, Peanut, and Pinecone, thanks for continued support and for playing Pup Patrol as I write this between naps. Thank you for allowing me to get excited about things and getting excited along with me.

To my extended family of authors, speakers, and opinion-givers. I love and appreciate all of you. Mom, thank you specifically for your terminology and encouragement. I hope your book sells a bazillion copies and you go on *The Ellen DeGeneres Show* and/or *Oprah*.

To Debbie Fay, Tiffany Zick, and Kelli (Webb) Medley, thank you for your support at each stage of my career. You provided the right mix of advice, encouragement, challenge, and (thankfully) willful ignorance of crazy ideas. I would not be the teacher I am today without your involvement and I'm better for having met you.

To the 900-something students I've had. I'm sorry that I didn't do more. When you're a teacher, you'll understand. Your best never feels like enough. Teaching is the hardest and best job in the world and I hope all of you (and your children) have excellent teachers who care about you as much or more than I do.

To Dave and Shelley, Erin, Genesis, Lori, Annie, Beth, and Liz. Thank you for your continued patience and teaching us how to be authors. You polished our rocky blog posts and stacked them into a book. Thank you.

Bring The Classroom Chef to Your School

You seem pretty cool. We'd like to meet you in person.

Visit ClassroomChef.com/reservations to request a full-day training, workshop, or just a day of chatting with your departments. However you want to make learning meaningful, we want to be a part of that conversation.

Become a Classroom Chef

It is our sincerest hope that you'll share your great ideas with the world of education. To create a place to do that, we've set something up for you:

ClassroomChef.com/recipecard

There, you can enter your own recipe card—like the ones you've seen in this book—and browse through recipes submitted from others.

MORE FROM

Dave Burgess Consulting, Inc.

Teach Like a PIRATE

*Increase Student Engagement, Boost Your
Creativity, and Transform Your Life as an Educator*
By Dave Burgess (@BurgessDave)

Teach Like a PIRATE is the New York Times'
best-selling book that has sparked a worldwide
educational revolution. It is part inspirational
manifesto that ignites passion for the profession
and part practical road map, filled with dynamic
strategies to dramatically increase student
engagement. Translated into multiple languages,
its message resonates with educators who want
to design outrageously creative lessons and transform school into a life-changing experience for students.

Learn Like a PIRATE

*Empower Your Students to Collaborate,
Lead, and Succeed*

By Paul Solarz (@PaulSolarz)

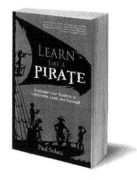

Today's job market demands that students be
prepared to take responsibility for their lives and
careers. We do them a disservice if we teach them
how to earn passing grades without equipping
them to take charge of their education. In Learn
Like a Pirate, Paul Solarz explains how to design
classroom experiences that encourage students
to take risks and explore their passions in a stim-
ulating, motivating, and supportive environment
where improvement, rather than grades, is the focus. Discover how student-led
classrooms help students thrive and develop into self-directed, confident citizens
who are capable of making smart, responsible decisions, all on their own.

P is for PIRATE

Inspirational ABC's for Educators

By Dave and Shelley Burgess (@Burgess_Shelley)

Teaching is an adventure that stretches the imagination and calls for creativity every day! In *P is for Pirate*, husband and wife team, Dave and Shelley Burgess, encourage and inspire educators to make their classrooms fun and exciting places to learn. Tapping into years of personal experience and drawing on the insights of more than seventy educators, the authors offer a wealth of ideas for making learning and teaching more fulfilling than ever before.

Play Like a Pirate

Engage Students with Toys, Games, and Comics

by Quinn Rollins

Yes! School can be simultaneously fun and educational. In *Play Like a Pirate*, Quinn Rollins offers practical, engaging strategies and resources that make it easy to integrate fun into your curriculum. Regardless of the grade level you teach, you'll find inspiration and ideas that will help you engage your students in unforgettable ways.

eXPlore Like a Pirate

Gamification and Game-Inspired Course Design to Engage, Enrich, and Elevate Your Learners

By Michael Matera (@MrMatera)

Are you ready to transform your classroom into an experiential world that flourishes on collaboration and creativity? Then set sail with classroom game designer and educator, Michael Matera, as he reveals the possibilities and power of game-based learning. In *eXPlore Like a Pirate*, Matera serves as your experienced guide to help you apply the most motivational techniques of gameplay to your classroom. You'll learn gamification strategies that will work with and enhance (rather than replace) your current curriculum and discover how these engaging methods can be applied to any grade level or subject.

Pure Genius

*Building a Culture of Innovation and
Taking 20% Time to the Next Level*

By Don Wettrick (@DonWettrick)

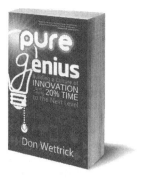

For far too long, schools have been bastions of boredom, killers of creativity, and way too comfortable with compliance and conformity. In *Pure Genius*, Don Wettrick explains how collaboration—with experts, students, and other educators—can help you create interesting, and even life-changing, opportunities for learning. Wettrick's book inspires and equips educators with a systematic blueprint for teaching innovation in any school.

The Zen Teacher

Creating FOCUS, SIMPLICITY, and TRANQUILITY in the Classroom

By Dan Tricarico (@TheZenTeacher)

Teachers have incredible power to influence, even improve, the future. In *The Zen Teacher*, educator, blogger, and speaker Dan Tricarico provides practical, easy-to-use techniques to help teachers be their best—unrushed and fully focused—so they can maximize their performance and improve their quality of life. In this introductory guide, Dan Tricarico explains what it means to develop a Zen practice—something that has nothing to do with religion and everything to do with your ability to thrive in the classroom.

Master the Media

*How Teaching Media Literacy Can
Save Our Plugged-in World*

By Julie Smith (@julnilsmith)

Written to help teachers and parents educate the next generation, *Master the Media* explains the history, purpose, and messages behind the media. The point isn't to get kids to unplug; it's to help them make informed choices, understand the difference between truth and lies, and discern perception from reality. Critical thinking leads to smarter decisions—and it's why media literacy can save the world.

The Innovator's Mindset

Empower Learning, Unleash Talent,
and Lead a Culture of Creativity

By George Couros (@gcouros)

The traditional system of education requires students to hold their questions and compliantly stick to the scheduled curriculum. But our job as educators is to provide new and better opportunities for our students. It's time to recognize that compliance doesn't foster innovation, encourage critical thinking, or inspire creativity—and those are the skills our students need to succeed. In *The Innovator's Mindset*, George Couros encourages teachers and administrators to empower their learners to wonder, to explore—and to become forward-thinking leaders.

50 Things You Can Do with Google Classroom

By Alice Keeler and Libbi Miller
(@AliceKeeler, @MillerLibbi)

It can be challenging to add new technology to the classroom, but it's a must if students are going to be well-equipped for the future. Alice Keeler and Libbi Miller shorten the learning curve by providing a thorough overview of the Google Classroom App. Part of Google Apps for Education (GAfE), Google Classroom was specifically designed to help teachers save time by streamlining the process of going digital. Complete with screenshots, *50 Things You Can Do with Google Classroom* provides ideas and step-by-step instructions to help teachers implement this powerful tool.

140 Twitter Tips for Educators

Get Connected, Grow Your Professional
Learning Network, and Reinvigorate Your Career

By Brad Currie, Billy Krakower, and Scott Rocco
(@bradmcurrie, @wkrakower, @ScottRRocco)

Whatever questions you have about education or about how you can be even better at your job, you'll find ideas, resources, and a vibrant network of professionals ready to help you on Twitter. In *140 Twitter Tips for Educators*, #Satchat hosts and founders of Evolving Educators, Brad Currie, Billy Krakower, and Scott Rocco offer step-by-step instructions to help you master the basics of Twitter, build an online following, and become a Twitter rock star.

Ditch That Textbook

*Free Your Teaching and Revolutionize
Your Classroom*

By Matt Miller (@jmattmiller)

Textbooks are symbols of centuries of old education. They're often outdated as soon as they hit students' desks. Acting "by the textbook" implies compliance and a lack of creativity. It's time to ditch those textbooks—and those textbook assumptions about learning! In *Ditch That Textbook*, teacher and blogger Matt Miller encourages educators to throw out meaningless, pedestrian teaching and learning practices. He empowers them to evolve and improve on old, standard teaching methods. *Ditch That Textbook* is a support system, toolbox, and manifesto to help educators free their teaching and revolutionize their classrooms.

Your School Rocks...So Tell People!

*Passionately Pitch and Promote the
Positives Happening on Your Campus*

By Ryan McLane and Eric Lowe
(@McLane_Ryan, @EricLowe21)

Great things are happening in your school every day. The problem is: no one beyond your school walls knows about them. School principals Ryan McLane and Eric Lowe want to help you get the word out! In *Your School Rocks...So Tell People!*, McLane and Lowe offer more than seventy immediately actionable tips along with easy-to-follow instructions and links to video tutorials. This practical guide will equip you to create an effective and manageable communication strategy using social media tools. Learn how to keep your students' families and community connected, informed, and excited about what's going on in your school.

How Much Water Do We Have?

5 Success Principles for Conquering Any
Change and Thriving in Times of Change

by Pete Nunweiler with Kris Nunweiler

In *How Much Water Do We Have?* Pete Nunweiler identifies five key elements—information, planning, motivation, support, and leadership—that are necessary for the success of any goal, life transition, or challenge. Referring to these elements as the 5 Waters of Success, Pete explains that like the water we drink, you need them to thrive in today's rapidly paced world. If you're feeling stressed out, overwhelmed, or uncertain at work or at home, pause and look for the signs of dehydration. Learn how to find, acquire, and use the 5 Waters of Success—so you can share them with your team and family members.

ABOUT THE AUTHORS

John Stevens is an educational technology coach and has had the honor of presenting around the country at various technology and math conferences. He has taught high school geometry, algebra 1, middle school math, service learning, and robotics, engineering, and design since 2006. He has earned the reputation as the go-to guy for trying new, crazy, and often untested ideas to see how well they will work. In 2014, he joined the group of Google for Education Certified Innovators.

He co-founded and moderates #CAEdChat, the weekly teacher Twitter chat for the state of California. John maintains a site called *Would You Rather...?*, which is asking students to make a choice and justify their reasoning with math. He is an author of *Flipping 2.0*, a resource that helps teachers take the flipped classroom to the next level. John blogs at Fishing4Tech.com. His latest adventure has led him into the world of 3D printing and designing lesson plans and curricula. Strike up a conversation on Twitter @jstevens009 or email him at stevens009@gmail.com.

Matt Vaudrey is the educational technology coach for Bonita Unified School District. He presents his forward-thinking teaching approach at conferences throughout California. He has taught eighth grade, seniors, and most math classes between. Recently, his school tagged him to pilot a 1:1 iPad program for intervention students. With no curriculum, Matt sought ways to make math meaningful for his students using free technologies available.

Matt blogs at MrVaudrey.com and connects with educators across the world on Twitter @MrVaudrey. He takes any opportunity to talk shop with other teachers, which may be why his Mullet Ratio has been used (and improved upon) by teachers around the world. Do you have an unusual idea? Matt wants to hear it and help make it fantastic.